BIRDER'S

BREAK

ALSO BY GERRY RISING

The Nature Watch Collection – Book One

The Nature Watch Collection – Book Two

Birds and Bird Watchers

AND AS GERALD RISING

Letters to a Young Math Teacher

Program Your Calculator

Inside Your Calculator

About Mathematics

BIRDER'S BREAK

by

Gerry Rising

W. R. PARKS
Hershey, PA

ISBN-13: 978-1983923142

ISBN-10: 1983923141

Library of Congress Control Number: 2018900711

Published by William R. Parks

Hershey, Pennsylvania

WRParksPublishing@gmail.com

www.WRParks.com

Twitter: www.twitter.com/WParksPublisher

Facebook: www.facebook.com/wparkspublishing

Cover

The spectacular cover photograph of a great horned owl was taken by my friend, Dick Collins, an international award-winning wildlife photographer. For more about Dick's photographs see Wild Side Photographic Art on Facebook.

DEDICATION

I dedicate this book to those young men and women, especially those who are teenagers and even younger, who separate themselves from the crowd, as I did, to become birdwatchers, and for whom the cry, "Look! Look!" is not a trick to divert attention, because there really is a tanager in that tree or a kettle of hawks circling those clouds.

INTRODUCTION

Birders have lots of between-times. A flight to Alaska to pick up the latest Asian avian wanderer to visit North America. An evening at a motel waiting for tomorrow's guided visit to the Michigan pine barrens to observe Kirtland warblers. Hours on the clacking and shuddering train riding north to James Bay to visit the summering grounds of birds we normally see only during their occasional winter visits to the states. Pre-dawn minutes waiting in a Montana blind for the grouse to arrive and strut around their lek. A long sit at a hawk watch when the winds turn northerly. A winter snow day, the blizzard outside preventing your trip to the Niagara River to seek out the visiting California gull. Or just waiting to be picked up by a fellow birder on a promising spring morning. This book is offered to fill those between times. It can fit a ten-minute stop or a few hours pause.

These hundred brief essays also represent the kind of reading I enjoy myself when I have a break. You can pick and choose or read them in sequence: there are no order requirements. They also represent a personal lifetime of birdwatching and study of avian ecology.

But they also represent the interpretations of an amateur. I am like most of you: a birdwatcher whose vocation was very different but who has devoted thousands of hours to the field study of birds. Beginning when, as a 10-year old, I was drawn to the challenge of bird identification, my interest grew during my school years through fortunate associations with remarkable men (for birdwatching was then essentially a male activity) like Gordon Meade, Allan Klonick, Joe Taylor, Howard Miller, Fred Hall and Tom Killip. My ornithological activities dipped during my four-year World War II navy service, but they picked up again when I returned to college and continued as a teacher. That interest matured through my career in education and now my over twenty years of retirement from university teaching.

In no way do I pose as an ornithologist, but during those years I served my time on various natural history and conservation boards, as president of the Genesee Ornithological Society and as editor of the New York State journal, *The Kingbird*. In 1955 I initiated the state's annual January waterfowl count, now as I write in its 48th year. Many of these essays are revisions of articles initially prepared during my twenty-five years writing weekly "Nature Watch" pieces for the *Buffalo News*; some appeared more recently in *Buffalo Spree* and other publications, and a number are here for the first time.

In these informal essays then I share with you readers my own wide-ranging avian interests. I hope you find among them many that will prove of interest to you as well.

Gerry Rising
January 2018

TABLE OF CONTENTS

1. Freeze

The slight duck-like horned grebe had been diving for minnows outside Buffalo's Small Boat Harbor breakwall for several days. Each time it dived, it did so with a spring out of the water and a graceful arcing twist back in bill-first. With this impetus it dived down thirty feet into the murky depths, using its short wings as well as its oddly-lobed feet for propulsion, literally flying through the water. Seconds sped by as it searched for a school of fry. Finally catching sight of dimly flashing fins, it darted toward them to seize one. Then up, up, up until it finally broke the surface and refilled its lungs with air. It had been underwater for more than two minutes.

The grebe was in winter plumage. The gray of its back continued up over the top of its head in contrast with the white of its cheeks, throat and sides. It retained from its summer coloration of rich chestnuts only the bright red eye at the border between gray and white. The thin sharp bill made it apparent that this was not a duck.

This was a bird of the year. It had been raised last summer on a reed nest in a Quebec marsh north of the St. Lawrence River. Now just months after it had ridden gaily on its mother's back it faced an immediate threat to its life because Lake Erie was rapidly freezing over! What had been an open expanse of water was now increasingly covered with ice that was rapidly coalescing into a solid surface. The grebe had to take off to search for open water while there was still the twenty yards it needed to beat its way awkwardly into the air.

The awkward flier just made it before the ice closed in and now it found itself rising over a vast ice sheet into swirling winds and snow. In the sub-zero temperatures the entire east end of the lake had suddenly frozen and the bird could only hope to find an opening elsewhere. But visibility was terrible. With only white in all directions and no evidence of even a dim sun, the bird became disoriented and changed direction several times.

Then through the white mist the grebe made out a dark line of water ahead and turned down to land. Just as it realized its error it hit the asphalt road and bounced into a snowdrift at its edge. It was uninjured but completely helpless. It couldn't even move penguin-like on land and it simply struggled limply in the deep snow. If one of many predators — cat, dog, fox, skunk, raccoon, coyote — did not find it, it would soon die of exposure and starvation.

And here it came. A shadow loomed over the grebe and it found itself grasped in firm hands, pulled from the drift and placed inside a dark box. The bird's physiological systems came to its defense: its reactions slowed, it no longer struggled. In shock it had no realization that it was being carried by car from Hamburg where it was picked up, across the Skyway into Buffalo and finally along Niagara and Ferry Streets to Squaw Island.

Now everything happened fast. It was light again and those firm hands held the grebe out over the largely ice-free Niagara River. Coming out of its shock as it was released, it flapped to the water and found itself in its own element once again.

This horned grebe had no idea that this story with its happy ending was being repeated hundreds of times with the assistance of wildlife rehabilitators, conservation department personnel and other caring individuals.

Unknowing how fortunate it had been, the little grebe merely prepared for another dive.

2. Charles Sibley and the Woodpeckers

Over my lifetime we have witnessed some remarkable paradigm shifts in science. Perhaps the best known is the acceptance in geology of plate tectonics, the idea first offered by Alfred Wegener that the surface of the earth is divided into large regions that shift over time. For example, eons ago Africa and South America fit together like jigsaw puzzle pieces. (Although Wegener first presented this idea in 1912 well before even I was born, it was not widely accepted until the 1960s when new evidence was brought to bear in support of it.)

Another striking change has been in the basis for classification of all living things on Earth, on the so-called Tree of Life. You may recall your school biology book illustrating the various life forms by this tree diagram with larger branches representing divisions like plants and animals, offshoots standing for groups like families and genera while the outermost twigs are finally species like scarlet tanager, common buttercup, monarch butterfly, gray fox, sea cucumber, E. coli and, yes, Homo sapiens a.k.a. you or me.

Until about forty years ago this diagram was not only considerably less complicated (it didn't separate bacteria, for example) but it was determined largely on the basis of similar physical structures. For example, lineages among animals with skulls could be determined partly by differences in their jaws.

Classification today is instead largely based on molecular biology: DNA differences separate those Tree of Life branches. While the genetic analysis largely confirms the earlier physical divisions, many differences have been discovered. If, for example, you look at a modern bird field guide, you find the order of species presentation unlike that of earlier guides. In my first bird book the loon appeared on the first page, the bluebird on the last. Now the loon follows all the waterfowl and even the game birds. And about a hundred species — all the warblers, for example — follow the bluebird.

I had the great good fortune of enjoying the friendship of one of the first ornithologists who worked on this reclassification. In a journal article I defended a widely criticized position taken by Charles Sibley and he wrote to thank me. Based on this encounter we developed that friendship and corresponded as he continued his work at Cornell and other universities until his death in 1998. According to his *Wikipedia* entry: "He had an immense influence on the scientific classification of birds, and the work that Sibley initiated has substantially altered our understanding of the evolutionary history of modern birds."

I feel that I was especially fortunate because Sibley remained a controversial figure with an acid tongue. According to his friend Richard Schodde, "Lesser mortals were not tolerated easily and, as has been said by others, collegiate friends were few." I saw instead the gracious side of this famous scientist and I was deeply saddened by his death.

I thought of Sibley when I read an interesting 2009 technical paper in *The Condor* by Amy Weibel and William Moore about downy and hairy woodpeckers. I am convinced that Sibley would have been delighted to read it. I cannot recommend it to non-scientists, however, as it is rife with technical language including jaw-locking words like synapomorphies, intron, homoplasies, clade and dimorphism. I offer here my take on that interesting essay.

If you have a bird feeding station, you surely know these two woodpecker species, the hairy and the downy. At a distance they are not at all easy to tell apart. The hairy woodpecker is slightly larger than the downy and has a larger bill; except for a feather or two, however, that's it for differences. Males of both species have a red dot on the back of their crown. The only species I know that look more alike are the alder and willow flycatchers that even banders cannot differentiate. (Birders identify the two by their calls; banders simply call them Traill's flycatchers.)

It turns out, however, that these two woodpeckers belong to distinct groups and tracing back along their branches, you pass through three divisions for the downy and two for the hairy before you reach a common ancestral limb. Although this is a bit like tracing your own genealogy back to your forebears, these ornithological branches each stand for many generations.

Thus these two look-alikes represent what is termed convergent evolution: two different branches leading to twigs with similar characteristics. Other examples of convergent evolution are monarch and viceroy butterflies (also appearance), bats and birds (flight), porcupines and hedgehogs (quills) and koalas and humans (fingerprints).

Weibel and Moore trace how the woodpeckers' physical characteristics changed in parallel with their molecular changes, some turned on and then off over time, but finally leading to this remarkable similarity

What caused this final convergence? The authors offer several possibilities related to flocking, aggression, and territoriality but these remain untested hypotheses. Molecular analysis provides no help at all here.

3. Winter Field Birds

Through the winter three unusual sparrow-sized bird species are seen with some regularity feeding in farm fields near the Lake Ontario shoreline. They are horned larks, snow buntings and Lapland longspurs.

Horned larks occasionally nest here — remarkably beginning in March when snow still covers many fields — but all three are better known as birds of the very far north. A spring trip to Moosonee on James Bay or Churchill on Hudson's Bay offers the opportunity to see them actively raising families.

These birds often travel together in mixed flocks and their numbers vary through the winter months. Snow buntings are most common from Thanksgiving to Christmas and in late March when large numbers of them migrate along the lake. Flocks of hundreds and even as many as several thousand are occasionally to be seen rising from fallow fields, in the distance the mostly white buntings looking like a cloud of wind-blown snowflakes.

Smaller groups remain through the winter and even in the harshest storms you can count on seeing a few dozen if you search for them here. Birders do this is by watching farmers spreading cow manure on their open fields. Scanning a steaming area of newly spread manure will often disclose these birds. They are also drawn to roadsides where they pick up grit, which substitutes for teeth in their digestive processes.

My experience with them has, until this year, been restricted to views at a great distance through a powerful telescope. My eyes tearing in the wind, I can barely make them out. Even at high power, they are usually scarcely more than dots in the lens and the light reflected off the snow plays tricks with my vision. Under these conditions, separating the rarer longspurs from the larks and buntings poses an almost impossible problem.

But then a few days ago, Mike Galas, Bill Watson and I saw them in a new way.

We had spent the morning looking unsuccessfully for rough-legged hawks and short-eared owls along the Ontario lake plains and we stopped to order sandwiches and coffee at the delicatessen in the village of County Line on Route 18. We then drove a few hundred yards into Niagara County and pulled off the road to eat. Birds often feed in the field to the north and as we ate we hoped to watch them from the car.

Sure enough, soon a flock of several hundred birds appeared, many of them snow buntings but with a good number of horned larks among them. They were moving slowly across the fields just beyond some farm buildings. At perhaps fifty yards this was as close as I had ever seen them.

Because we stayed in the car, our presence had no effect on the birds and slowly a number of them moved still closer. A single bird would fly a few yards, several would follow, then still more would trail along. Within a few minutes many were within twenty yards.

Closest of all were the horned larks. Even without binoculars we could see their delicate black facial markings and the tiny cowlick feathers that give them their name.

The accompanying snow buntings were still in winter plumage and the males did not yet show their black-backed breeding attire. On the ground they displayed only a little brown and gray against the white, but whenever they flew we could see their black wing tips.

Finally here came three Lapland longspurs, more sparrow-like in appearance. In summer the males have a black crown, face and breast, but now the sexes look much alike. Brown streaked birds, more sparrow-like in their appearance, their buffy ear patches served as identifying marks. Whenever the flock rose in flight the longspurs were easy to pick out: they were the darker birds.

Not soon again will I see these attractive birds up so close.

4. Listing

To birdwatchers competition takes the form of listing. Most active birders I know keep life lists of species identified; many go on to keep year and month lists, as well as May "Big Day" lists. They also keep local lists, state lists, some even world lists. And they compare with each other. "How many species have you seen so far this year?" "How many warblers did you get yesterday?" are common inquiries.

I am not foreign to this competing. Without looking it up I can tell you that my year high in western New York was 258 species in 1988 when I tied Mike Galas and Dick Collins. The next year Dick and Mike did still better.

Notice that only part of that competition is with others. More of it is with oneself. At least a dozen local birders have seen more species here than I have in a year, but for many years that did not take away from my annual effort to reach 260: to improve, as that movie title has it, my personal best. Now as my hearing, eyesight and skills deteriorate I have to push hard to reach 200 and this year with an operation scheduled I will be fortunate to make 150. But to a newcomer to birding the goal of reaching a 100 species life list holds the same excitement.

Some birdwatchers disdain listing as frivolous. On the other hand some of the most respected ornithologists — Ludlow Griscom, James Fisher, Roger Tory Peterson, for example — regularly compiled such lists.

Like the 3.45 minute mile and the 20 foot pole vault, there are benchmark numbers that listers try to meet or break. One of those local marks is 100 species in January. In 1989 Dick Collins, Mike Galas, and I just made it to that total, at the time a local record. But in 1991 Willy D'Anna shattered that record by seeing 105 in January, a spectacular total — something like adding a foot to the pole vault mark.

In an article in *The Prothonotary*, the journal of the Buffalo Ornithological Society, D'Anna describes his achievement as a product of luck, assistance from friends who called his attention to hard-to-find species, and a mild winter. I would add to that modest assessment, persistence, many long and exhausting days in the field and most of all his excellent skills.

To achieve a high total in January you must see almost all the birds that are usually found in the region at that time of year. Then you must find a good number of additional unexpected species, birds seen here in milder seasons but rarely in winter.

Some unexpected species D'Anna found were: tundra swan, snow goose, ruddy duck, ring-necked duck, common black-headed gull, black-legged kittiwake, Forster's tern, yellow-bellied sapsucker, and Eastern towhee.

In mid-January D'Anna found his 99th species on the Statler Building, a hotel in downtown Buffalo. It was a peregrine falcon, one of those rare predators that teetered on the brink of extinction when DDT still worked its insidious effects up through the food chain. Its numbers have been enhanced through a process called hacking, but peregrines are still uncommon.

Then on January 18, he counted 100, again in the city. Quite remarkably it was another rare falcon: a merlin. Ellen Schopp helped him locate it in a pine grove on the University at Buffalo Main Street campus.

After that, he says, everything was anticlimactic.

Like an outstanding achievement in sports, D'Anna's record will spur others to set their sights high. And this competition will add to our ornithological knowledge of the Niagara Frontier through the more intensive fieldwork demanded. One factor that will encourage competitors is the complete absence of winter finches from D'Anna's list. In a year when they were in the region he could have added another six species!

Of course you always miss at least one bird you count on. D'Anna's nemesis was cedar waxwing.

5. Fuertes and Audubon

In his 1937 *Natural History Magazine* paper titled "Fuertes and Audubon — A comparison of the work and personalities of the world's greatest bird artists," Frank Chapman tells about a personal experience: "On one occasion, in William Brewster's museum, calling Doctor Coues' attention to the published drawing of a small bird by Audubon, I said: 'Doctor Coues, if this drawing were brought you today for publication, would you accept it?' His reply, 'Audubon was Audubon and the account is closed,' expresses the attitude which the world at large still holds in regard to the paintings of birds by John James Audubon."

Chapman then goes on, however, to "open the account," with the qualification, that he does not "question the magnitude of Audubon's achievements. Beyond question he was the greatest painter of birds the world had known." But he then asks, "Is that a reason why his fame should obscure that of those who followed him and who, through their greater gifts and because of the inspiration derived from his works, have surpassed him in his chosen field? To believe that Audubon still holds the exalted position of the world's leading painter of birds is to admit that there has been no advance in the art of bird portraiture in the past one hundred years. It would be equally untruthful to say that we know no more about the habits of birds at present than we did in Audubon's day."

In the remainder of his essay, beautifully illustrated with Fuertes' drawings and paintings including the one at the beginning of this essay, Chapman establishes how Fuertes work improved upon that of Audubon. He concludes his account with, "Each was the greatest bird painter of his day. Each was inspired by standards that defied time and strength and patience and was satisfied only when he had given his best. But the standards of Fuertes' day, reflecting the developments of a century and the criticism of his associates, were the higher and to him was given the power to meet them."

I suspect that many readers of this essay will have no familiarity with Fuertes' art. That is unfortunate because I believe that he deserves the recognition that Elliott Coues, a leading ornithologist of the early 20th century, was to assign him while Fuertes was still a young man: "I say deliberately, with a full sense of my words, that there is now no one who can draw and paint birds so well as Mr. Fuertes, and I do not forget Audubon himself when I add that America has not before produced an ornithological artist of equal possibilities."

Louis Agassiz Fuertes (1874-1927) was closely associated with New York State. His father was an engineering professor and later dean at Cornell University. The boy first drew domestic animals, but then, according to a brief autobiographical sketch he wrote later, "About 1888, when 14 years old, L.A.F. made his first essay at painting a bird from the flesh in his boyhood home at Ithaca, N. Y. It was a male Red Crossbill — the first that he had ever seen, and the strange coppery brown of its plumage, its unbelievably queer bill, its sturdy little figure all claimed something that had never before been fully awakened. So, to fasten these peculiar qualities in his mind, where they could be retained, he followed the method that first suggested itself, and which he has followed ever since — he drew and painted it to the best of his power."

His art improved until as a Cornell undergraduate Fuertes was introduced by a fellow student to Elliott Coues, one of the founders of the American Ornithologists Union and at that time editor of that organization's journal, *The Auk*. Coues recognized Fuertes' talent, promoted him to his AOU colleagues and provided him with both commendations and instructive criticisms of his art. For example, in one letter to his protégé, Coues wrote: "I have your 16 new drawings. They are beauties indeed. You seem to improve with each new effort.... I heartily approve this lot, with no criticism except in one case. You must do the Turnstone over again. It is good, but not up to your present mark; for you have relapsed into your early crudeness about the belly and legs."

When Fuertes' parents became concerned about their son's future occupation, Coues wrote to his mother calling her attention to his estimate of Fuertes as exceeding Audubon in talent and adding, "I have sometimes fancied his father was not altogether pleased, or even satisfied, and imagined he had other plans for his son's future. But if Louis' gifts be what I believe them, he will never make anything of himself, except along the lines of their exercise and development — never attain to more than 'respectable mediocrity' (which for me means dead failure) in any other direction." Needless to say, both parents were more than satisfied with this encouragement and gave their son their full support in his choice of vocation.

Upon graduating from Cornell Fuertes spent a year apprenticed under the artist Abbott Thayer, who served as a great influence on the technical aspects of his painting. Thayer is best known by naturalists as a proponent of camouflage and in particular counter-shading, the effect that a light source has on darkening objects in shade. Almost all bird species have lighter colored breasts than backs to neutralize this effect. The bobolink represents a rare exception.

The remainder of Fuertes life was rich and varied. He contributed hundreds of sketches, drawings and paintings to books and magazines. He went on expeditions with senior ornithologists to Florida, Alaska, Texas and New Mexico, the Bahamas, the Yucatan, Columbia and Abyssinia. He taught and lectured at Cornell.

Although his paintings include birds found on those international trips, his two best-known collections are those that appear in Elon Howard Eaton's 1910 *Birds of New York* and Edward Howe Forbush's 1927 *Birds of Massachusetts and other New England States*. Those paintings have served thousands of birdwatchers and me in particular very well as detailed plumage references.

Sadly Fuertes life was cut short when his car was hit by a train shortly after his return from Abyssinia. His wife survived the crash as did the paintings he had prepared for Forbush's second edition.

Chapman concludes his extraordinary obituary of Fuertes with these words about the artist as a companion: "He was never wanting; he never disappointed you. From start to finish he was a stimulating scientific associate, and an enthusiastic, helpful comrade. He multiplied your joys and shared your sorrows. He could handle mules or jefe politicos with equal success. He was collector, artist and cook in one. He was never too tired for fresh exertion, never too discouraged to try again. He got the best out of every experience whether it was a new bird, a view or some minor incident of the day's work. No one could resist his ready wit, his whole-souled genuineness, his sympathetic consideration, his generosity of thought and deed. Everywhere he made new friends and everywhere he found old ones. He never seemed to get beyond the range of Cornell men. They might be classmates or recent graduates, but to them all he was 'Louis' and the glowing warmth of their greeting bespoke the depth of their affection."

Notes: Much of the information in this essay is drawn from Chapman's obituary in *The Auk* 45 (1): 1-26 and from the paper noted in the first paragraph which may be accessed at: archive.org/stream/naturalhistory39newy#page/205/mode/1up. Fuertes' owl drawings included with this essay are taken from that publication. I commend these articles to you and for the best of his North American bird portraits to Forbush's *Birds of Massachusetts*.

6. Early Spring Waterfowl

It will be several weeks before concentrations of Canada geese and other waterfowl draw us to the Iroquois National Wildlife Refuge. Today those swamps are vast stretches of snow-covered ice with very little open water. A visit there last week turned up only one lone coot paddling around a hot tub-sized pool.

But there are many ducks here already. In fact you have the opportunity in early March each year to observe some of our most handsome wild birds. And not only can you see them, but you can see them up close, so close that you won't even need binoculars.

To enjoy this experience, simply cross the Peace Bridge and drive or hike north along the west side of the Niagara River. The river edge is attractive parkland almost all the way from Fort Erie to Niagara-on-the-Lake so, except for the mile or two at Niagara Falls, you will have generally unobstructed views of the water.

Although there are the usual dabblers — mallards, black ducks, Canada geese and even some tundra swans off Navy Island — most of the ducks you'll see here are diving ducks. For those who don't know the distinction, let me explain.

Dabbling ducks are those that feed in shallow water, tipping up their tails as they dunk their heads down to the bottom to harvest plant life. They rarely submerge their entire bodies. Geese and swans also feed in this same way. Diving ducks, as their name implies, plunge well beneath the water surface. Although sportsmen often consider all diving ducks fish eaters, with the exception of the mergansers their diet includes very few fish. The divers also feed on plants and their proportionally smaller animal diet is supplied mostly by mollusks, crustaceans and water insects.

A few days ago Mike Galas, Bill Watson and I found twelve species of diving ducks along the river and there will soon be several more. With an identification guide, you would have little trouble distinguishing these striking birds.

All along the river are the most common wintering divers: greater scaup ducks — the hunters' bluebills. (Their bills are indeed a soft Wedgwood blue.) It will be a few more days before lesser scaup ducks will return from the south to pose identification problems.

Smaller flocks of goldeneyes and the diminutive buffleheads usually stay apart from the other species, but individual common and red-breasted mergansers mix right in. We found a single hooded merganser as well. A careful search might even turn up the rare harlequin duck: a single female was just offshore behind the restaurants in Fort Erie.

Rafts of several hundred canvasbacks with a few redheads among them are to be seen between Frenchman's Creek and Chippewa.

But the best is still to come. After you descend the Niagara escarpment you begin to see long-tailed ducks, the snow buntings of the waterfowl world. They are largely white ducks, showing varying amounts of gray on their breasts and sides. Just as at this time of year snow buntings fly back and forth over open fields, these ducks rise in similar groups to fly up and down the river. Males have long central tail feathers and for this reason hunters call them sprigtails.

Much as I enjoy watching these lovely birds in flight, I look forward even more to approaching a flock that is gathered on the water. Then you understand where their earlier politically-incorrect name oldsquaw originated. They are quite simply gossips. Eager to tell each other the latest dirt on their own Caitlyns and Bernies, they gabble in their soft melodious voices, their comments overlapping in their eagerness to get their stories out first.

As usual it is the females who get the blame assigned in that name, but as in our human case the males are full and equal participants.

The name of the oldsquaw duck was changed in 2000 to long-tailed duck by the American Ornithologists' Union. Although this name change was partly and rightly to avoid the negative connotation of the word squaw to Native Americans and all women, it was also to bring the name into alignment with that of other countries.

7. Tower Kills

If you look ahead when you drive south from Buffalo, New York at night, you can see red lights winking high above the ridges. Easily mistaken for low flying aircraft, they are instead lights on the transmission towers for local television stations. We pay little attention to those towers, and neither do some of the birds migrating south through this area – to their misfortune.

Early in the morning one late September I drove up from South Wales on Warner Hill Road and Center Street to visit those TV towers. It was the beginning of a beautiful early fall day, the broad cloudless sky a bright blue in the rays of the newly risen sun. To the northwest the hills gave way to a broad plain extending off to blue-gray Lake Erie. At its corner downtown Buffalo appeared in miniature.

I had never realized how high these towers reach. Even though the sky appeared cloudless, each of them disappeared into a thin mist and I could not see the tops of their red and white scaffolding. And no wonder. A sign at Channel 7 recorded the altitude at that point as 1735 feet and the tower height an additional 1076 feet. These TV structures are like 80 story buildings erected atop hills already the equivalent of 100 stories above downtown Buffalo. For comparison, our tallest Buffalo building at 529 feet, Marine Midland Tower, has 40 stories, and the tallest self-supporting structure in the world at that time, Toronto's CN Tower, is the equivalent of about 140 stories. (As this is written, the world's tallest building is the Burj Khalifa in Dubai, United Arab Emirates, at 167 stories.)

The reason for the great height is apparent. It allows these stations to broadcast their straight-line television signals to every home in western New York and nearby Canada. But those metal structures and their associated reinforcing cables create problems for nocturnal bird migrants. I was visiting the towers with Arthur Clark, curator of vertebrate zoology for the Buffalo Museum of Science, to record some of the birds that had flown into them.

Art has kept track of nocturnal avian migrants killed at these towers for 30 years and this year has been one of the best for his records, which he adds, "means one of the worst for the birds." This fall he has picked up well over 300 at the tower bases. Almost certainly at least that many more fell into the deep grass nearby or were carried off by scavengers.

We had no sooner gotten out of our car at the first tower when we came upon a pile of perhaps a dozen tiny feathers, all that remained after a great horned owl had breakfasted on the bird's body. As Art gathered the few feathers carefully into an envelope, he identified them as coming from a black-and-white warbler. To me this also identified Art Clark as an ornithological Sherlock Homes. The best I could do was call it "a small bird."

We found about 50 more birds at the three towers, including many other warblers and vireos, a few thrushes and sparrows, and a catbird. Almost all of the bodies had been ravaged by local horned owls, for which these fields serve as autumnal smorgasbords.

Why do birds hit these towers? This is a difficult question about which Clark is only willing to speculate. Two possible answers: the towers and cables may be struck at random by individual birds in much larger flocks or the required aircraft warning lights may disorient or even attract them. (Perhaps someone should climb up some night to gather first hand evidence. Any volunteers?)

No one likes to witness the death of birds at these necessary structures, but the birds' demise at least provides this fine scientist with evidence about nighttime migration patterns.

An article titled "Faulty Towers" in the September-October 1996 issue of *Audubon Magazine* honored Clark for his 35 years studying this problem. The author of the article, David Malakoff, tells of visiting Art's walk-in freezer in his small museum lab. "There behind the remains of a seven-foot sturgeon caught in nearby Lake Erie and those of a young gorilla from a zoo, were stacks of carefully labeled boxes. They held most of the 20,514 tower-killed birds Clark has collected since he started his tower study in 1967."

A full-page photograph shows Art holding the body of a brown thrasher behind boxes containing dozens of other species.

"Once researchers might have dismissed Clark's collection as merely an ornithological oddity," Malakoff continues. "But it now offers compelling evidence in a growing debate over the threat that the nation's 75,000 radio, television, and cell-phone towers pose to birds, particularly to the 300 or so species that migrate by night."

The article concludes: "Meanwhile, Art Clark is preparing for another season of pilgrimages to his towers. It is unglamorous work — hauling the folding ladder he uses to check for bird bodies on rooftops and getting someone to mow the fields so that the casualties can be found. Not so long ago he considered giving it up, because the task was getting expensive and producing fewer specimens for his museum. Now, though, he's...looking forward to those occasionally cloudy morning commutes. 'It's getting exciting,' he told me recently. 'It would be wonderful if all this effort eventually helps solve the problem.'"

Art has long been retired from his curatorial position at the museum but his specimens and records remain for further analysis.

8. Hunter's Stand

While hiking recently, I came upon an example of modern technology supporting sport. It was a spanking new, metal hunting stand mounted against a big beech tree. The beech tree was, of course, provided by the accommodating forest.

Like anyone who has spent time in the woods, I have seen hunting stands before. Usually they amount to a few boards or sticks nailed to a tree so that the hunter can climb to a low limb or fork. There he or she will stand or sit for hours, often cold and uncomfortably cramped, in wait for game. Sometimes the stands are more complex, perhaps a few more boards providing a kind of tree house, but never before had I seen anything as smart as this. Although this stand was made of aluminum, it still must have taken some effort to pack it in to this remote glade.

In appearance this stand looked like half of a children's slide — the stairs half. The steeply slanting gray steps were fastened to the tree with braces and straps midway up and at the top.

I climbed up these steps carefully — my purpose education, not vandalism. Reaching the top I clumsily turned and seated myself on the comfortable cushion. There were even seat belts. They would be a must for someone like me: if I spent any time in this cozy position I would surely fall asleep.

It was a delightful spot. I could see about 80 yards in three directions through the mixed open forest. There were generally big old trees that shaded out undergrowth. In addition to the predominant beeches and maples there were tuliptrees and basswoods and a few spruce whose lower limbs had died back leaving them standing like feather dusters among the thick table legs of the bigger hardwoods. The forest floor was leaf covered, providing a background of somber but not unattractive yellows and browns. Only the spruces offered a contrasting green.

As I sat for a few moments, a troop of small birds moved into the area and advanced from branch to branch nearby. They paid me little attention and it was a special pleasure to be with them up here in their world. First appeared a silent brown creeper hitching its way up a tree trunk. It was soon joined by noisier birds: chickadees whistling their high-pitched notes and *dee-dee*ing; a downy woodpecker wheeling to call *pick* at me as it flew past and then whinnying from a dead snag; and a nuthatch, whose nasal *yank yank* suggested a severe adenoidal problem. A sentinel blue jay screamed from the higher branches. And finally I made out, well down the slope just where the trees began to blend together, a more reticent hermit thrush perched on a low branch.

Within minutes the 15 to 20 birds were gone and the woods were again silent. Reluctantly I climbed down and hiked on.

I am not a hunter but I have many friends who are. This brief experience reminded me of my friend, Don Nelson, who constructed and began using a makeshift stand in the Adirondacks. There he encountered birds from his lookout just as I had. Intrigued by them, he began carrying bird seed in his pocket and was soon able to feed small birds from his hand. Unable to identify the birds, he bought a field guide, carried it with him, and began to discover what species visited him in his forest hide. He knew he was hooked on bird watching, he told me, when on one trip he discovered after sitting on his tree limb for almost an hour he realized that he'd left his gun at the base of the tree.

9. Blame It on Shakespeare

As you might expect, there are many lines in Shakespeare's plays that refer to birds. Here are a few of my favorites:

A lover's eyes will gaze an eagle blind.
— Love's Labors Lost
True hope is swift, and flies with swallow's wings.
— Richard III
A very fox for his valor. —
True, and a goose for his discretion.
— Midsummer Night's Dream
I am but mad north-north-west.
When the wind is westerly, I know a hawk from a handsaw.
— Hamlet

(There is an odd twist to that last. It is usually interpreted as the Dane's claim that he is at least at times not insane: he knows a bird from a carpentry tool. The statement may have a less extreme reference, however; what is recorded as "handsaw" may have misrepresented the word "hansa," at the time a common name for heron.)

A few years ago I used a Shakespeare concordance to seek out more of these avian references. I found hundreds of them and now I learn that a French scholar, Pierre Acobas, has found even more. He lists on his "Shakespeare's Ornithology" website a total of 606 occurrences of bird names for 64 species. Most often mentioned is dove which appears 60 times with runners-up: goose 44, eagle 40, crow 38, owl 36, hawk (including falcon) 35, and nightingale 30.

All of that information is worth only a footnote were it not for a single ornithological quotation that has had a profound effect. In Henry IV Part 1, the king orders the soldier Hotspur never to mention the name of his brother-in-law Mortimer again. This does not sit well with Hotspur who thinks:

He said he would not ransom Mortimer.
Forbade my tongue to speak of Mortimer,
But I will find him where he lies asleep,
And in his ear I'll holla "Mortimer!"
Nay, I'll have a starling shall be taught to speak
Nothing but "Mortimer," and give it him
To keep his anger still in motion.

That is the single mention of the bird we in the Americas know as the European starling (*Sturnus vulgaris*) in all of Shakespeare.

*

So what?

Here's what. Jump ahead from the time that was written three hundred years to a cold and snowy March 6, 1890 in New York City's Central Park. A group of people descend on the park carrying small cages containing sixty birds that have been shipped across the Atlantic at great expense. The cages are ceremoniously opened and their contents — sixty starlings — are released.

Unaccustomed to their new surroundings the birds fly to nearby trees where a few of them are attacked by shrikes. To save the starlings the shrikes are shot.

Knowing what we do today you might think that the people releasing those birds represented a foreign nation seeking to do violence to our own. Quite the contrary, they were representatives of The American Acclimation Society, a group led by a pharmaceutical manufacturer, Eugene Schieffelin, who sought to introduce to the United States all the bird species mentioned in Shakespeare. They wanted to enhance the quality of life here by bringing us as many of those 64 species as possible.

Of course very few of the ones new to this country, like the nightingale and the British robin, lasted more than a few days, but two made it, as they say, in spades. The other "success story" was the house sparrow (*Passer domesticus*). In 1858 Schieffelin had already introduced those birds to his New Jersey garden where they flourished.

Today Schieffelin and his followers are considered at best eccentric, at worst insane, but at the time his work was well received. In fact William Cullen Bryant wrote a poem celebrating his introduction of the house sparrow. Here are a few of its 36 lines:

> *A winged settler has taken his place*
> *With Teutons and men of Celtic race;*
> *He has followed their path to our hemisphere*
> *The Old-World Sparrow at last is here....*
> *The insect legions that sting our fruit*
> *And strip the leaves from the growing shoot,*
> *A swarming, skulking, ravenous tribe,*
> *Which Harris and Flint so well describe*
> *But cannot destroy, may quell with fear,*
> *For the Old-World Sparrow, their bane, is here.*

Clearly Bryant was no ornithologist for the house sparrow diet was quite unlike what he suggested, but the house sparrow did indeed flourish.

Even more significantly, those starlings and their offspring spread across North America. Until 1900 their range was restricted to metropolitan New York City, but by 1913 they had reached western New York. By the 1920s they were recorded in the Midwest, the 1940s the west coast and the 1970s Alaska. It is estimated that their North American population peaked at about 150 million. (Their global population is 310 million.)

These birds do a significant amount of agricultural damage. They consume cultivated fruits like strawberries, apples and cherries, damage ripening corn, eat livestock grain, pull and eat sprouting winter wheat and damage golf course turf. Their large roosts also produce noise, odor and filthy, corrosive and even slippery accumulations of droppings. The annual cost in the United States of their activities has been estimated at $80 million.

In addition starlings represent a management challenge at airports: in 1960 a Boston aircraft collided with a starling flock, the resulting crash killed 62 passengers.

Finally they severely impact native cavity-nesting birds such as bluebirds and woodpeckers for nest sites. Here on the Niagara Frontier they have, for example, been a primary cause of the near-extirpation of red-headed woodpeckers.

All this from those few birds introduced in a New York City park two hundred years ago.

Although it is clear that we must live with starlings and house sparrows, it is worth noting that the population of both species has declined since their numbers peaked. Bird counts indicate that our starling population has decreased more than 50%. House sparrow numbers are even more reduced from the early 20th century when we traveled by horse-drawn carriages and these birds fed on their droppings. They also met a competitor when native western house finches moved into the eastern states.

In fairness I conclude this essay by noting that there is one time of year when I appreciate starlings. It is in early summer when they march in line across our lawn picking out beetle grubs.

10. Hunters and Wildlife Watchers

It seems unfortunate to me that a gulf is too often identified between participants in the outdoor sports — hunting and fishing — and those who take part in nature-related activities, the wildlife watchers — birders, botanists, hikers, conservationists, nature photographers, Audubon members and the like.

Although many of my recreational activities identify me as a wildlife watcher, I have many good friends who are hunters and anglers. Of course we kid each other: to them I'm a "tree hugger," "lily collector" or "dickeybirder" and I remind them that they are "bloody carnivores" or "scatter-shots." However, we find remarkably few issues on which we disagree.

We each want to conserve our natural areas. We are each concerned about those who misrepresent us: those trespassers, litterers and poachers who give us all a bad name and as a result force landowners to post their property. We are each concerned about those animals and plants that are increasing out of control: Canada geese, swallowwort, starlings and house sparrows, purple loosestrife, zebra mussels, mute swans, common reed, tent caterpillars, white-tailed deer and Japanese knotweed. We're equally concerned about the decline or loss of other species: grouse, wild orchids, red-headed woodpeckers, American elms and chestnuts and black ducks and blue-winged teal.

Yes, hunters do shoot turkeys, pheasants, ducks, rabbits, squirrels and deer; and trappers kill muskrats, mink, foxes and other furbearers. Those are animals and birds that I enjoy watching. But I recognize that their hunting and trapping is monitored and controlled by federal and state conservation regulations so that wildlife populations are not threatened. And I also recognize that we need some of the controls that hunting and trapping exact.

Consider, for example, deer. While I appreciate the beauty of deer, I also appreciate the beauty of wildflowers. Deer and wildflowers are today completely out of balance. In many of our woodlands you will find very few wildflowers. In fact you will find little undergrowth from the ground up to about five feet. That is a direct result of deer overbrowsing.

It is easy to demonstrate this effect. Exclosures, areas enclosed by high fences, have been built to do so. Within months there is a profusion of growth inside the fence in marked contrast to that outside.

In any case we nature lovers don't have to *support* hunting and fishing to *cooperate* with those who do so on the ventures on which we agree.

Here's an example of what we can achieve together: I have served with outdoor sportsmen on the board of the Friends of Iroquois National Wildlife Refuge, the group that led the replacement of the Swallow Hollow Trail, a three-quarter-million dollar project. It is important to note that the trail provides no access whatsoever to hunting yet the hunters pitched in to support the project with no hesitation.

Even more important to all of us concerned about wildlife, over the years outdoor sportsmen and women nationally have contributed to the purchase or lease of wetland habitat over $700 million through purchase of duck stamps. That has meant the protection of over 8,000 square miles, an area about equal to that of New York State west of the Genesee River.

Remember, those lands are open to hunting for only a few weeks each year. Meanwhile, all year long they provide much needed habitat to all kinds of wildlife.

As a first cooperative measure, I urge my wildlife watching friends to start paying our dues. We too should buy duck stamps or what they are now called, Migratory Bird Hunting and Conservation Stamps. You can purchase one for $25 at most post offices.

As I write, the current stamp pictures trumpeter swans, favorites of mine since I first saw a pair of them flying along the Yellowstone River in Montana.

Today we wildlife watchers outnumber all hunters and anglers together. We could make a huge contribution to the kind of land acquisition and protection that we need today.

Many years ago when I was president of the Genesee Ornithological Society in Rochester, I was asked to represent the society on the Monroe County Conservation Council. I accepted the invitation and spent several years as a member. They were very rewarding years.

At first I was uncomfortable at the meetings. Before my appearance the Council membership was entirely drawn from the hunting, angling and trapping communities. As almost anyone will attest, being a newcomer at meetings of people you do not know is not easy, but in this setting I faced more serious difficulties. I represented a community usually identified as opposed to everything these people stood for. And I did indeed oppose some of their views.

Recognizing my discomfort, however, the Council's leaders went out of their way to accept my presence and I soon was recognized as the group's token tree-hugger. In fact when that designation was used (as it would be later by Mike Levy at the *Buffalo News*), it was always with an accompanying grin. But that kidding helped accommodate me.

And what soon became apparent was the fact that we agreed on many issues. Despite their negative reputation among many of my personal friends, these men and women I soon realized were not the enemy. This was where I learned that roster of agreements I listed earlier.

Of course our views diverged on some sensitive issues and our minds were rarely changed on those issues. But over time both they and I realized that our communities were not represented by the extremists that so often characterize us. These were not people who believed that their second amendment rights entitled them to carry flame throwers and howitzers into local grocery stores. And, although our motivations differed, I was as concerned as they were about the actions by animal rights extremists. Their concerns centered on hunting-related actions, mine on Animal Rights proponents' attacks on research facilities and their support for feral cats.

Even when we differed and retained our differences, we at least heard each other out. And because my council membership worked out so well, over time representatives of other organizations, among them the local Burroughs Audubon Nature Club and the Rochester Museum of Science, were invited to that conservation council. Mine then was no longer a lone voice.

Now I live in a community where no Council like what I described exists. Because of my Rochester experience, I recognize how much we lose by this absence. Both groups would have a much stronger voice if they worked together and rarely have I seen them do so.

Consider a recent issue here in New York State. Soon after a school shooting, the state issued a series of gun-related rules under the rubric, the SAFE Act. Of course, we birdwatchers and botanists loved the legislation; the hunters hated it. I personally took this opportunity to talk to some hunters about their concerns and I learned that there were two quite different reactions to the act. The first was rejection of any legislation that restricted the use of firearms in any way. In this they echoed the response of the National Rifle Association, whose posture on any gun-related issue is "never retreat." But many of my friends had less universal concerns. They found flaws in the bill that needed to be addressed: for example, some sections applied unequally to what were essentially equivalent firearms, thus punishing individual owners. I found their concerns reasonable and was prepared to support them and I believe others of my community would have done so as well. How much better it would have been in their attempt to modify the law for the "gun crowd" to have had us birders on their side? I am convinced that many hesitant legislators would have been prepared to listen, given that independent support for changes.

At the same time I believe that we are losing on land conservancy issues because we don't have hunters with us.

If we had such an organization, we might be able to reach some compromises and, even if we did not, we could gain insights into and appreciation for our opponents' motivations.

11. Hurricane Birds

Hurricanes are oceanic events. It is over open water that they build up their tremendous power. That violence most often affects us when they first come ashore, because, once their path takes them inland, that power is rapidly dissipated. But some of those storms still carry high winds and heavy rain well beyond the coast. In August 1955, for example, the effects of Hurricane Connie continued all the way to Algonquin Park where I was on a canoe trip. There were so many trees blown down that crossing portages was like climbing through a child's Jungle Jim.

We have problems with wind damage and flooding, but birds too are seriously affected. Here are my observations of some of the effects of Hurricanes Connie, Fran and Isobel.

The phone call came on a September evening in 1996. It was Bob Brock, my informant at that time on the Buffalo Ornithological Society Rare Bird Network. Usually his call would tell me the name and location of an unusual species that had turned up on the Niagara Frontier. I would make notes and pass on the information to those next on the list.

This time the call took longer — he was reporting eight rare birds. All had been seen across the Niagara River along the Lake Erie northern shoreline. And all were marine species that almost never venture inland. They had been brought to this region in the eye of Hurricane Fran, that strange calm center of a tropical storm that is surrounded by raging winds. For these birds it was an enforced trip of over 500 miles.

One was a laughing gull whose distinctive *ha ha ha* call is familiar to coastline residents but seldom heard here. Three related species joined it: Sabine's and Franklin's gulls and several sooty terns. Harrying them and the local ring-billed gulls were two long-tailed jaegers, piratical seabirds but splendid falcon-like fliers.

Rarest of all were a black-capped petrel and a Wilson's storm-petrel, two gull-like birds of the open ocean. They have strange tubes on their upper mandibles that contribute to sensory functioning. Even though I once joined a pelagic trip especially to observe one and spent months at sea during World War II, I have never seen a petrel.

Rounding out the list was an American oystercatcher, a big, thick-set black and white shorebird with a huge red bill about which I write brefly in essay 23. Although it is fairly common along Long Island beachfronts, I know of only one previous record for this species in the entire Great Lakes region.

Only after these remarkable storms are such birds found inshore. After Hurricane Connie passed through this area, for example, a storm-petrel appeared at Greg Sommer's Long Beach cottage. He picked up the exhausted bird and placed it in his birdbath. The bird drank briefly and then surprisingly flew away. The other species stand a good chance of returning to their oceanic environment, but unfortunately the petrels will almost certainly die. They won't find squid, their favored food, in Lake Erie.

We were lucky with Hurricane Fran. There was no flooding or beach erosion here, but our beaches at that time were strewn with the detritus not only of summer storms but also of human carelessness.

Buffalo meteorologist Steve McLaughlin described Hurricane Isabel as the "non-event" of September 2003. This serious storm was perfectly forecast as it hit the mid-Atlantic coast but turned a bit further west than expected as it approached western New York, tracking over eastern Ohio and Lake Erie instead.

My visit to Alexandria, Virginia that month confirmed for me how fortunate we were to have missed the fury of this vicious hurricane. Three weeks after the storm passed through that area, clean-up operations were still underway. The suburb my brother and I toured had been inundated by water driven from the Potomac River. It had reached five feet in the living rooms of some homes and ruined furniture was still stacked everywhere waiting to be picked up by sanitation trucks. Some of those same homes had also gone for weeks without power. One early estimate would make this the most costly hurricane until then, its expense exceeding the $26.5 billion of Hurricane Andrew in 1992. Of course this was dwarfed by the later cost of 2011 Hurricane Katrina at $145 billion.

Indeed, we not only had the good fortune to be missed by the storm but some birdwatchers were rewarded by its approach. They flocked to the shores of Lakes Erie and Ontario to look for exotic species brought by Isobel, even though it had been downgraded to a tropical storm: the possibilities including petrels and shearwaters, jaegers and gannets, as well as unexpected species of gulls and terns.

I joined Bob Andrle, Fran Rew and Joe Thill at Hoover Beach in Hamburg for a few hours one sunny afternoon several days after the storm bypassed us. A strong on-shore westerly wind was blowing and the blue water of Lake Erie was creased with whitecaps. There were few birds out over the lake; most of the local gulls relaxed in troops on the beach. Others had retreated much farther inland.

After a long search Bob was able to follow one storm-petrel for several minutes in his telescope. Despite his careful instructions, however, the rest of us could not find the swallow-sized bird flying a quarter-mile out over the lake.

Other observers were more fortunate and Wilson's, Leach's and black-capped storm-petrels, parasitic jaegers, black-legged kittiwakes and least, sooty and elegant terns were reported in the region. Farther afield were additional species like bridled and royal terns, laughing gulls, black skimmers, band-tailed storm-petrels and greater shearwaters.

Sadly, the petrels would die within a few days. Unlike land birds (and us) the physiology of many waterbirds is specially designed to accommodate them to seawater. They have salt glands that reduce the concentration of salt to levels their digestive systems can manage, the separated brine drooling back out from their bills. But for some reason these birds are unable to survive over fresh water like our Great Lakes.

These storms have another far less entertaining effect. They add to the litter that gathers on the beaches over which they pass. Of course the operative word there is "add" for we litter those beaches even more than the storms do.

I urge readers wherever you are to join your annual Beach Sweep that is scheduled each year in late September. The Great Lakes Beach Sweep of which ours is a part has now been extended to coasts and riversides in 43 states and 72 countries. Although this activity is sponsored by the American Littoral Society, the state Department of Environmental Conservation, the Center for Marine Conservation and dozens of local organizations, Sharon Trembath continues to be the moving force here. For her this is a year-round activity that culminates in this massive two-hour effort.

In one recent year forty tons of trash were picked up in New York State by 5000 volunteers.

12. Rachel Carson

"There was a strange stillness. The birds, for example —
where had they gone? Many people spoke of them, puzzled
and disturbed. The feeding stations in the backyards were
deserted. The few birds seen anywhere were moribund; they
trembled violently and could not fly. It was a spring without
voices. On the mornings that had once throbbed with the
dawn chorus of robins, catbirds, doves, jays, wrens, and scores
of other bird voices there was now no sound; only silence lay
over the fields and woods and marsh."

Do you recognize that quote? Sadly, I am sure that today
few will know of it. It is one of the key paragraphs from
Rachel Carson's evocation of a future dominated by pesticides
in her paradigm-shifting book, *Silent Spring*. I join many who
consider that book in a special class of influential volumes
together with Darwin's *Origin of Species* and Harriett Beecher
Stowe's *Uncle Tom's Cabin*. (About the latter recall Abraham
Lincoln's comment upon first meeting Mrs. Stowe: "So you're
the little woman who wrote the book that started this great
war.")

It comes as a shock to me to realize that *Silent Spring* was
first excerpted in *The New Yorker* magazine and then
published as a book in 1962. That is over a half century ago
and today most middle-aged adults can only view the episode
as a kind of historic artifact. To me and to many others of my
age, however, the book's remarkable immediate influence and
the storm of controversy occasioned by its publication
represent a defining time in world-wide conservation history.
Translations were soon published in seventeen languages. As
just one example of its international impact, in 1963 a five-
hour debate in the British House of Lords was devoted to
Carson's claims with copies of her book to be seen in the
hands of many members.

Let me take you back to those times as I recall them.

DDT is an important pesticide that probably saved hundreds if not thousands of lives of soldiers fighting in the South Pacific during World War II by suppressing the clouds of insect carriers of malaria and other diseases. After the war it and other even more powerful insecticides like Endrin were used to destroy neighborhood mosquitoes and, more important, crop-destroying pests. Everyone who lived in this country then witnessed clouds of insecticides spread by airplanes and trucks or individually by spray cans. Ad campaigns — one even showing a man drinking DDT — promoted the safety of these chemicals.

But problems were becoming evident. The pesticides killed not only harmful insects but their predators — wasps and birds, for example — as well. Also, over time the harmful insects built up physiological defenses against the poisons. This was leading researchers to develop more potent chemicals and users to rely on more and more of them.

Another aspect of the problem was even more threatening. The pesticides had persistent, long term effects and they became more potent up the food chain. A robin feeding on infected earthworms absorbed more of the poison and homeowners began to witness robins undergoing the same death throes that insects went through. Of course, a hawk feeding on birds like that robin ingested still more of the poison. Animals and birds high up in the food chain especially suffered: eagles, ospreys and peregrine falcons were disappearing from the landscape. We too live high in the food chain and people began to worry about their effect on us as well.

There were also episodes of major kills. For example, millions of fish turned belly up in the Mississippi River near a plant that developed Endrin. The association could not be made, however, because at the time instruments were not powerful enough to detect the very tiny amounts of poison it took to kill a fish, less than one part in 100,000.

There were, of course, vested interests (with their lobbyists) who strongly supported the use of pesticides. The major players were the chemical companies that were researching, developing and manufacturing the chemicals. But they were not alone. Governmental and academic agriculturists strongly supported their use. Some of the strongest critics of *Silent Spring* were professors from agricultural colleges like Cornell. Yes, there was self-interest here, because the chemical industry was supporting them with major grants, but many of these academics and governmental agents sincerely believed that withdrawal of the chemicals would allow valuable crops to be destroyed. They were also afraid that their withdrawal would allow diseases like malaria to spread.

The inevitable result was that virtually nothing was being done to address the problem.

Enter the remarkable Rachel Carson who is a perfect example of a person who does not hold a doctorate but who is better qualified to speak out than many who do. Her education included a Johns Hopkins zoology master's degree, but she was forced to abandon her doctoral work there when her father died and she found herself responsible for her family. She became an aquatic biologist at the United States Bureau of Fisheries.

Carson was a wonderful writer who had her early essays published from the age of ten. She earned a national reputation for an extremely popular book, *The Sea Around Us*, which not only won the 1952 National Book Award for Nonfiction and the Burroughs Medal but also remained on the *New York Times* Best Seller list for 86 weeks. I highly recommend this book and its two companions, *Under the Sea Wind* and *The Edge of the Sea*. They represent the most beautiful nature writing you will ever encounter. Their success allowed Carson to leave her government work and to reside in Maine at that sea edge she had described in her book.

There her concerns about pesticides were focused by her observations of the effects of widespread spraying.

As she worked on *Silent Spring*, Carson found many scientists who supported and contributed to her efforts. A master at translating science retained from her government work, she was careful in all but that first allegorical chapter to provide scientific support for her claims about pesticide effects. But she allowed her argument to flow by relegating that support to 53 pages of notes at the back of her book.

The reception of the book made headlines around the world and battle lines were immediately drawn. I salute in particular President John Kennedy for his support of Carson's work. He charged a President's Science Advisory Committee to investigate her claims and to report to the nation. The report strongly supported *Silent Spring*. Here is a statement that characterizes it, "Elimination of the use of persistent toxic pesticides should be the goal."

That did not, of course, end the matter and it took years to implement at least some of the President's Committee recommendations. But the world today is far different from what it was before *Silent Spring*. Today eagles and ospreys and even peregrine falcons have returned.

There is a heroic aspect of Rachel Carson's story. As she was completing work on *Silent Spring* in early 1960 her doctor found lumps in her left breast and a mastectomy was performed. Unfortunately, although the doctor had considered the procedure precautionary, by December it was determined that her cancer was malignant and had metastasized. Thus, despite being weakened by her treatments, this courageous woman finished work on the book and stood up to and largely dispelled the storm of reaction. She died finally in April 1964 at age 57, less than two years after her seminal book was published.

13. Duck Story

I am going to tell you about the most embarrassing moment in my life.

My suburban Rochester high school class was the World War II class of 1944, but I sneaked out at the beginning of that year to enlist in the navy on my 17th birthday. Happily for me, the navy had the good sense to realize that they would be taking a real chance sending this moral coward out to fight so they sent me instead to college, in fact to the University of Rochester five miles from my parents' home.

And that is why I returned for a day in 1945 to that high school to talk to the students. I had been invited to serve on a panel speaking to the student body about what we graduates were doing that was unusual. I have no idea why I was chosen. I was considered by most of my teachers and especially by my athletic coaches to be barely mediocre. Probably those ahead of me on their list all turned them down flat. At any rate I foolishly accepted the invitation.

Now I was left with problems. First, what should I talk about? That was at least reasonably easy. I was a birdwatcher. Ornithology would do. Never mind whether my teen-age audience would have any interest in this subject.

I organized some facts that interested me about birds — never even considering whether they would communicate anything to my audience. I stitched those facts together into a kind of short speech.

But now I faced a serious problem. I had heard that it was important for a speaker to capture his audience's attention with a strong opening sentence.

An idea came to me. I had found in my reading that about six billion birds move north over the United States each spring during migration. I also learned that about sixty million of those birds are waterfowl. I glued those facts together and had my opener.

I still seriously considered canceling my appearance, but I had forgotten the name of the administrator who invited me so I showed up on the appointed morning. It was a warm day in early May; even so I was freezing with stage fright.

We were organized backstage. Around the edge of the curtain we could see the audience gathering. Talk about a reluctant crowd. They were dragooned into assigned rows by bored teachers who then headed for the nearest exit. The crowd that remained was a surly looking lot.

After all of them had found their assigned seats they slouched to their feet to sing an off-key rendering of our national anthem. The principal said a few smarmy words and we took our positions at the table to mild and clearly unenthusiastic applause.

Without me my colleagues had caucused beforehand to make me go first. Introduced by the principal, I rose and moved reluctantly to the podium. This was it.

I paused — not dramatically: fear had congealed my muscles. But my standing there immobile had an unusual effect on the audience: the room went entirely silent and for that brief moment I had everyone's full attention. Finally, over the expectant hush I took a deep breath and carefully articulated into the microphone my introductory statement.

My voice boomed out over the auditorium enunciating that opener I had so carefully designed as an attention getter:

"One out of every one hundred birds is a duck!"

That opening was received by a second or two of absolute silence. But this was followed by a quite unique and unexpected reaction. First titters but then a huge roar came up from the audience. Gales of laughter. Applause.

Stunned, I just stood there. Behind me one of my fellow speakers laughed so hard he tipped over his chair.

The noise went on for minute after minute. A few times it would seem that things were quieting down and I would get ready to go on only to have giggling start and then the laughter would again sweep through the audience.

Now during the brief pauses wags began to shout out their own turns on my phrasing. "One out of every 100 cows is a horse," one yelled and another called back a more rational, "One out of every 1000 teachers is a human being." These brought new screams of laughter.

After what seemed like hours of this misconduct the principal came out. I could see that he was not only angry at the students, but at me as well — why me? I thought — and he sought to quiet the audience with the usual threats: detentions, cancelled events. But these students were not about to listen to reason. I had somehow caught this audience in an unguarded moment and touched something elemental in their psyche. What I said was, of course, not really humorous — it was simply mundane and ridiculous — but it somehow spoke to those kids on that particular morning.

The rest of the episode is too embarrassing even to recount. Students, still shouting with laughter, being marched out of the auditorium by their returning teachers. An apoplectic principal. My co-panel members giggling their thanks for heading off their own insipid presentations. The counselor who had invited us whispering to a colleague, "I knew he wasn't going to work out. Who the hell suggested him?" I slinked out the side door.

That day was, of course, one of the worst in my life. It ended, however, on a less somber note. Barely able to suppress tears, I drove out of the parking lot. As I passed the front of the school building, I noticed a lone student leaning out of a window of the school library. When he saw me driving by he waved and called out. His shout wafted down across the broad green lawn with its crisscrossing gray sidewalks. I could just make out his words: "Come back any time!"

14. Dawn Chorus

When I awake it is full dark. Far off the dog that has barked most of the night continues to cry wolf. This minor discordance accents the silence nearer by. Not even frogs croak.

What has awakened me is expectation. The luminous dial on my watch shows 4:30. What friends call the dawn chorus will soon begin; I think of it rather as an orchestra tuning up for the day ahead.

This is a wonderful way to enjoy the experience. I lie here in bed beside two wide-open windows of my in-laws' north Alabama home and simply listen. The gentle breeze makes it just cool enough for a light blanket. Today's low temperature will exactly match yesterday's reported high from Buffalo.

This house is on a dead-end road several miles outside the small town of Hartselle. Around its acre of lawn are fallow fields backed by woodlots running down to a branch called Flint Creek. The house itself is surrounded by many beautiful mature hardwoods, among them water oaks and a sweetgum. Directly outside this window are also a dozen long-leafed pines, several reaching seventy feet in height. There are only a few other houses and a small country church on this lane, none closer than a hundred yards.

Suddenly the silence is broken by a single coyote howl, immediately answered by a half minute of dog barking from neighbors' yards. This in turn awakens a cardinal whose notes calm the night watchmen.

I doze off in the ensuing silence only to be reawakened by a robin. He's the happy custodian of this rehearsal hall: his monotonous *cheery-up-cheery-chee* whistling will continue all day.

A rooster crows just once. Perhaps he's embarrassed because he's late with his wake-up call.

As I watch, the stars seem to wink off individually. Within minutes they are all gone and trees begin to take shape. On the other side of the house the eastern sky will be lightening. Dawn is on its way.

It is time for the players to test their instruments. A towhee chinks several times and then bows, *Drink teeeeea*, the second note a higher tremolo. Another cardinal whistles and a red-bellied woodpecker *churr*s.

In the drainage ditch across the road a spring peeper pipes its single clear note against a tree frog's background trill. From the same area a red-winged blackbird pumps its first *konk-a-ree*.

From the lawn edge a bobwhite tentatively sounds in perfect pitch only the *Bob* of its usual two-part call. Just as clearly, a titmouse contradicts him, *Peter, Peter, Peter*, from the neighbor's hedgerow.

A mourning dove coos in a lower register for a few moments, but something causes it to burst out of the pine and rush past my windows so closely that I can hear its wing beats. I don't know whether the jay's off-key shriek that follows is caused by the dove's sudden departure or the threat of the discovered predator.

Finally the soloists arrive. Catbird, thrasher and mockingbird test their repertoires from the now clearly visible shade trees, a wood thrush adding its organ tones from down near the creek.

Several players are missing this year. We're here earlier than usual and some have not yet arrived. Normally yellowthroats and indigo buntings would counterpoise their faithful repetitions to the variations of the mimic thrushes. And this year's bass section is deprived by the absence of its resident barred owl. I hope that it will be here when we next return.

Back in my Buffalo yard we have no orchestra, only a lounge trio: robin and dove with house wren as tympanist. I have to get up, dress and drive several miles into the countryside away from our sprayed and insect-'free' trees to enjoy a similar natural anthem.

15. Wildlife Rehabilitators

Carol Spann and her daughter Gail are wildlife rehabilitators. Together with eight volunteer assistants they operate Tri-County Wildlife Rehabilitation and Rescue Inc. in Attica Center.

To learn more about their work I spent a morning with Mrs. Spann at her old country home. Big shade trees surround the house and behind it is a small orchard, its trees now old and gnarled. When I arrived, my hostess was already out in mucking boots cleaning three carrying cages with hose and scrub brush.

Mrs. Spann is friendly and open, but there is also a no-nonsense, get-on-with-it quality to her. When she served me coffee and delicious brownies in her kitchen, I had the uncomfortable feeling that I was taking too much time from her work day that runs from dawn until well after dusk.

Rehabilitators, Mrs. Spann explained, accept orphaned, abandoned and injured animals and seek to return them to their wild state. Her center cared for 245 animals last year and this year she is certain that number will rise. Almost all but her permanent residents were gone, but a few weeks earlier she was caring for dozens of birds and beasts including a long tailed weasel and a wild turkey.

Their best-known patients this year were the young Oak Orchard ospreys that suffered from a severe virus and required weeks of care, including feeding and medication at 15 minute intervals day and night. Five of the seven were saved, one died and one escaped. But even that escaped bird is in good condition and is seen regularly in the Attica area.

Most of their charges are penned in the Spann backyard. One of the big flight cages held a Cooper's hawk that was almost ready for release. It flew from perch to perch when we looked in on it. In another cage was Alex the Great, a partially blinded great horned owl that clicked its bill ferociously at us; and in still another rested the silent Cheyenne, a regal red tailed hawk with a crippled wing. These last two can never be returned to the wild. Instead they serve as demonstration birds for Mrs. Spann's talks to sportsmen's clubs, church and youth groups and other organizations and her Genesee Community College rehabilitator license preparation classes.

Critical cases require care inside her home. An injured great blue heron stood quietly in a carrying cage in her dining room, waiting to be examined by Dr. Michael Bonda, the Orchard Park veterinarian. On the other side of the room were Nip and Tuck, two pet ferrets that had been taken by a game warden from an unlicensed owner. Mrs. Spann took Tuck from its hammock to cuddle in her arms while Nip lived up to its name by trying to bite my knuckle through the cage screen.

Like most rehabilitators, Mrs. Spann has also had her bathtub cases: grebes and loons picked up away from their normal lake habitat and this year an emaciated black duckling that at first would only feed in an inch of water.

Although mother and daughter both hold state and federal licenses and are regularly granted special permission to work with endangered species, Mrs. Spann is careful to describe their care as comparable to nursing. They are happy to work under the supervision of Dr. Bonda and in cooperation with conservation officers and wildlife biologists.

Their patients come to them from many sources. Too often a well-meaning individual picks up a wild animal, takes it home and then is surprised to find that it needs almost constant nurturing. Some people, Mrs. Spann laughed, don't realize that most animals are active at night. Eventually such animals usually arrive at her doorstep, often brought by policemen, but hunters and farmers also bring in animals.

I left Wyoming County with my already high regard for the wildlife rehabilitators of this region strongly reinforced. We're lucky to have people like the Spanns performing this useful voluntary function, their very considerable expenses only met personally and through direct contributions.

16. Honored Friends

Two stories.

The first was told to me years ago by Al Fudge of Elmira. One spring in the 1940s Al and his wife Vera were hiking in a Southern Tier forest when they met a young man who identified himself as Harold Axtell, a Cornell doctoral student studying the vertebrates (animals with backbones) of Chemung and Schuyler Counties. Al was impressed, he told me and I was too. Most doctoral theses are written about very narrow subjects — something like The Summer Distribution of Red-bellied Snakes in Delaware Park — but this young man had taken on a much larger problem.

Another thing that impressed Al was the fact that Axtell wore sneakers instead of hiking boots. Now his feet and trouser legs were soaking wet. When Al inquired about Harold's footwear, the young man replied, "I always wear sneakers when I'm hiking. My feet dry quickly and sometimes I learn from getting them wet. For example, in wading across that creek back there, I found the water colder than in other nearby streams. I have checked a topographic map and I'm sure that at the creek source about a half mile from here the temperature will be near freezing. That means that there is a real possibility of my finding there a rare red salamander, a species that prefers very cold water."

Naturally, Al told me, he and Vera were intrigued. With the young man's permission, they joined him in his climb to the stream source. Sure enough, there in the clear spring water were two beautiful red salamanders.

The second story is my own. Many years ago I rode in Joe Taylor's convertible with the top down. That would not be so extraordinary except that it was late December. We were on a Christmas census recording the birds around Braddock's Bay northwest of Rochester and it was bitter cold. Even with the layers upon layers of clothing I wore and even fortified by Helen Taylor's strongly seasoned and spiked bullion, I was finding the experience punishing. Not Joe: he had his jacket open and his shirt unbuttoned at the neck.

Suddenly he stopped the car. Across the reeds came the *two two two* cry of a lesser yellowlegs. We never saw the bird but it called several more times. Delighted at our find, we knew that it would be the best record of the day.

But when we reported this exceptional occurrence that evening at the census recording session, our coworkers laughed at us. They insisted that we must have heard the somewhat similar call of a pine grosbeak. One colleague even questioned how much of Helen's broth we had sipped. We argued but lost: our bird was not tabulated.

A month later, however, Walt Listman, on one of his regular forays into that same Braddock's Bay cattail edges, put up a yellowlegs. Our record may not have counted, but we knew that we were vindicated.

I have told those stories, because within a month both Harold Axtell and Joe Taylor died. Each was an honored friend for over forty years. Others have written of their great stature: Harold's service as zoology curator at the Buffalo Museum and his international reputation among field ornithologists, Joe's as president of Hawk Mountain Sanctuary and the American Birding Association and as one of the earliest members of the exclusive 700 Club of birders. Those aren't religious donors; they are rarer individuals: bird watchers who have identified 700 species in North America.

Their accomplishments were great, but I will remember Joe and Harold better for their personal qualities: their enthusiasm, their openness and most of all their willingness to share their vast knowledge of nature with so many of us.

And for me they will live on through our adventures together.

17. Our Attraction to Owls

What is it about owls?

That question occurred to me as I wandered through the Buffalo Museum of Science exhibit of award winning bird art where five owl paintings appeared among the other paintings and sculptures on display. An additional six owls were included in the show catalog. Artists are clearly attracted to owls out of all proportion to their numbers among birds. So too are the rest of us. But why? What is so special about these nighttime raptors?

To seek answers to these questions, I decided in the spirit of a recent election campaign to conduct a carefully designed survey. I asked four randomly selected people — who just happen to be my grandchildren — for their ideas.

"Why do you think we are so interested in owls?" I asked each of them by long distance telephone.

Marshawn, age ten, Denver: "They can turn their heads around and around." Well, not quite. Mike Galas and I tested this belief several years ago with a young great horned owl we found in an Iroquois National Wildlife Refuge woodlot. Mike walked around the owl while I watched. Owls' eyes don't scan as ours do. They must turn their heads to follow any moving object, so this owl's face followed Mike as he circled it. But just when Mike passed behind the trunk of the tree in which it was perched, the owl's head did a rapid near-360° reversal. To Mike the bird appeared indeed to be twisting its head off. From my vantage point I could see its trick.

Jordan, age seven, El Paso: "They're very wise." But consider James Thurber on this score. In his modern fable, *The Owl Who Was God*, Thurber tells of the secretary bird, sent to test the owl's intelligence, asking him, "How many claws am I holding up?" "Two," said the owl. "Can you give me another expression for 'that is to say' or 'namely'?" "To wit," said the owl. "Why does a lover call on his love?" "To woo," said the owl. When the secretary bird told others about these highly intelligent responses, the animals of the forest decided that the owl was God. Unfortunately, when in daylight the owl led the animals blindly down the highway, it could only respond when asked if it was afraid, "Who?" A truck ran them down.

Nicholas, age seven, Denver: "They come out at night." But so too do other less popular birds like swifts and whip-poor-wills. That criterion would also make moths more popular than butterflies, which is clearly not the case.

Lindsey, age four, El Paso: "What's an owl?" Unconcerned about my response she then chattered on about interesting but non-ornithological matters for ten minutes before she reluctantly gave up the phone to my daughter. In any case her answer disqualified her from the survey.

Lacking a fourth answer, I turned to my wife Doris, age not forthcoming, Buffalo, as a substitute. "They're sweet and cute," she responded, obviously referring to the little saw-whet owl we had found two years ago. She didn't recall the junco that owl had killed and hung from a nearby branch. Nor did she know about the great horned owl, that vicious midnight predator often rightly called the snapping turtle of the forest.

As you might expect, I came away from my survey with my questions still unresolved. What indeed is so special about owls? You'll have to seek for yourself an answer to this intriguing question.

18. Falcons

Falcons are aristocrats. Unlike slow-soaring buteos and darting, feeder-raiding accipiters; falcons are streamlined raptors whose long pointed wings drive them through the air faster than any other bird. They are the cheetahs of the skies.

The common falcon here is the American kestrel, which is — to use a term familiar to dog fanciers — a toy hawk. Its size is between that of a robin and a blue jay. At any time of year one of these diminutive orange-backed falcons with its helmet-like head markings may be seen perched on a phone wire or hovering over a meadow looking for large insects, mice or small birds.

Three other falcon species occur here, but all are uncommon. A recent visit of the largest and rarest of all, the gyrfalcon, is the reason for this essay.

The other two, the merlin and the peregrine falcon, are recorded here most years during spring migration and occasionally individual birds are observed in other seasons. For several winters a merlin regularly visited the University at Buffalo Main Street campus. And in each recent year peregrine falcons have been seen in downtown Buffalo and Niagara Falls. Occasionally one is observed perched atop a high building or sailing the canyons between towers, and Reverend Susan Cox recently reported a peregrine with a pigeon in its talons on a North Street sidewalk.

Gyrfalcons are seen here only about once in each decade. Their normal range extends across the northernmost reaches of Canada to the shores of Greenland and corresponding regions of the Old World. Only a few individuals retreat even to the southern areas of Canadian provinces in winter. Thus it came as a great surprise when two birds of this species were recorded along the Lake Erie shore a few years ago.

To better understand the size of a gyrfalcon, consider the progression from small to large falcon. The merlin is twice as heavy as the tiny kestrel, but it is still only pigeon-sized. The peregrine is over four times as heavy as the merlin. It is larger than a crow and its powerful appearance makes it seem larger still. Finally, the gyrfalcon averages another 75% heavier than the peregrine. It is a very large raptor, bigger even than a red-tailed hawk.

You can imagine the excitement then of Bob Andrle, Dean DiTommaso and others as they watched a big gray-phase gyrfalcon beating its way west toward the Erie shore near the end of Tifft Street. As it passed an abandoned grain elevator, the powerful gyr deigned even to acknowledge the peregrine perched on a high girder only a few yards away.

Feeding habits of the two large falcons differ, the peregrine often taking birds like pigeons on the wing, the gyrfalcon instead striking prey on the ground. In the northern tundra, its most common victims are ptarmigan, but it also takes lemmings, hares and sea birds even as large as geese. Early Arctic explorers, who carried pigeons for communication, reported that the gyrs could not catch these birds in flight, because the falcons' bulk did not allow them the necessary maneuverability; this suggests why they prefer surface hunting.

Gyrfalcons vary in coloration. White gyrs are prized by Arabian falconers, who employ them to hunt bustards, huge, slow-flying Old World birds that patrol open grasslands to feed on vegetation, small mammals and insects. Unfortunately the use of gyrs in falconry has attracted poachers all the way to Canada. In the United States the gyrfalcons are not as popular with falconers, partly because of their great expense but also because they do not respond well to training. Despite this, several years ago an escaped white gyrfalcon trailing a leg jess was observed in Buffalo.

The most recent unconstrained visitors from the high Arctic were brown and gray, but they still earned a royal welcome.

19. Birds for Elder Citizens

In her 86th year my mother developed an interest in birds. This started one night when a pigeon roosted on her nursing home windowsill. The next day she began to leave crumbs there to attract it back. When she told me about this, I gave my mother a container of bird seed and each morning she dutifully cleaned up the sill and placed a few new handfuls out "for her birds."

She loved to watch the birds, but she was especially happy about new ones that came to her makeshift feeder. Linnaeus or Darwin discovering a new species could hardly have been more excited. When we visited her, she would ask me to help her with identification. One day, for example, she greeted me with a detailed description: "It was beautiful," she said, "very small, with a black throat, gray bill and forehead and white markings on the cheeks. Its back was brown and it had one white wing-bar."

I showed her a picture in a bird book. "That's it!" she said and excitedly added that "beautiful" house sparrow to her list entitled "My Bird Friends."

I still retain that list. Even a neophyte birder would consider it pathetically short. It has on it only ten species, each with a single name: pigeon, sparrow, starling, finch, grackle, cardinal, dove, junco, chickadee and crow. The list would never have earned her a scout merit badge, but it gave her something far better: a new focus to her circumscribed life.

Only a few months later my mother fell and broke her hip. She never recovered. Her world closed still more tightly around her and she retreated into the Swedish speech of her childhood, unintelligible to us. But until then her birds replaced her so many friends who had died before her. And they gave her something to talk about to her few remaining human visitors.

I thought immediately of my mother's experience when Mike Levy told me about a program of the New York State

Department of Environmental Conservation (DEC) that provides bird feeding and observation opportunities for nursing homes.

Through this program service organizations that sponsor nursing homes are furnished a start-up kit that includes tube and platform feeders with 50 pounds of birdseed, a suet feeder with suet cakes, bird nest boxes, shrub and tree seedlings and a birdbath. As a wildlife bonus, a bat roosting box is also included.

n addition, the DEC provides a bird identification poster, two "how-to" guides for the sponsors and a brochure that tells about bird feeding and planting for wildlife. A video is included with the kit to help the nursing home residents identify common feeder visitors.

Initial development of this project was funded by the "Return a Gift to Wildlife" state tax write-off and twenty nursing homes are already participating. The closest to Buffalo are in Olean, Machias and Houghton. Mike Farrell of the Olean DEC Office is as enthusiastic as I am about this activity. Conservation officers like Mike provide continuing technical assistance to participants.

The $120 materials cost and on-site assistance is being provided by local service organizations that include hunting, fishing, 4-H, Rotary and garden clubs; as well as scouts and church groups. The New York State Ornithological Association is also supporting this activity.

Surely there can be few more simple, inexpensive and desirable community projects. The DEC and those public-spirited groups already participating are to be congratulated. I hope that others will contact their local DEC office to obtain more information and to sign on.

My mother would be pleased.

20. Breeding Bird Census

It was 4:55 a.m., still only half light. Our car was parked on the shoulder of Planck Road in Perrysburg. A pick-up truck had just passed and caught me in its headlights standing by the car door. The driver stopped, turned his truck, and came back. "Do you need help?" he inquired.

"No," I responded, "but I appreciate your concern. My wife and I are taking the annual breeding bird census of this area."

As so often happens, this farmer, whose property we would pass on our route, was genuinely interested in our project and informed about local wildlife. We chatted briefly before we drove off in our separate ways.

Doris and I were about to participate for our first time in what I consider the most significant annual birdwatching event, the Fish and Wildlife Service-sponsored June Breeding Bird Survey. We were just one of 17 teams in western New York and over 2000 teams in North America. Our route had been censused annually since 1967 by Bob Wagner and others. These carefully controlled counts monitor changes in breeding bird populations and represent the best available information on this important subject.

Marked topographic maps told us not only the roads to follow but also exact locations for each stop. To conform with past years we waited until exactly 5:10 a.m. to start our first count. Doris then clicked the stopwatch and I began to call out to her the birds I could identify: "Wood thrush. Yellow warbler. Veery. House wren. Ovenbird." This early I could respond only to songs; later I would see birds as well. Doris noted each individual carefully on her record sheets.

"Stop!" she called when three minutes were up. I climbed into the car and drove a half-mile to the next stop where we repeated our procedure. We did this fifty times on a route that took us 25 miles down country roads and through South Dayton until we finished at 9:40 just east of Cherry Creek.

It was a delightful experience. The early morning fog gave way reluctantly to disclose a bright blue sky. The countryside was at its best: open pasture and cropland with varying soft green shades, the contrasting deep greens of woodlots further accented by a few white wildflowers, well-maintained farm homes often shaded by giant pines, small alder and willow-bordered winding streams, and rolling hills that offered broad panoramas as we reached each crest.

It was an instructive experience too. The 56 species we recorded included two great horned owls, a cliff swallow, and at our very last stop a brown creeper. But what we didn't find was just as important: no brown thrashers, no vesper sparrows, only one bluebird. Would others have better luck with them? Our count will place a single piece into a nationwide jigsaw puzzle that would answer such questions.

Rich Wells, who maintains a 125-nest box bluebird trail in Springville, wrote recently: "No factor has more effect on nesting success of bluebirds than the weather. Cold wet weather makes it extremely difficult for adult bluebirds to brood their young and feed them insects. This spring southern Erie and northern Cattaraugus counties had some unusually cold weather with frost on May 25, 26, and 27. During this period I had 18 nestings of bluebirds with young ranging from one day to two weeks of age. Thirteen of these nests were completely lost (all nestlings) totaling 53 young. Five nestings were at least partially successful, losing ten young but fledging eleven. This is about a 30% success rate which is well below my seven-year total of 69%."

Individual experiences like Rich's provide drama and raise our consciousness; the F&WS surveys give us more prosaic long-term evidence. At this critical time both are very important.

21. The Best Singer

We each have our favorite bird songs. Among the birds of suburban gardens, for example, many of us would choose the cardinal, others the Baltimore oriole. In northern woodlands we might argue for hermit or wood thrushes or winter wrens. Pasture choices would surely include meadowlarks and bobolinks.

But which is best overall? That question was addressed by Charles Hartshorne in his 1973 book, *Born to Sing: An Interpretation and World Survey of Bird Song*. Hartshorne certainly earns high marks for seeking statistical support for this elusive — and very personal — question and it is easy to come up with questions about his results as I will shortly. Nevertheless it is interesting to consider both his method and his results.

Hartshorne's rating system is based on six criteria: loudness, complexity, time between songs, musical quality of the individual notes, overall musical quality and imitativeness. Each criteria is evaluated on a scale from 1 to 9 and the six scores are summed to assign a grade. For example, he assigns the bobolink, whose *spink-spank* calls enhance our meadowlands, 996984 for a total of 45, and the Henslow's sparrow, whose single *churp* suffices to announce itself, 311111 for a total of 8.

Here are his totals for some of the other birds of this region: hermit thrush 48, wood thrush 47, mockingbird and Carolina wren 46, brown thrasher and song sparrow 45, Eastern meadowlark 44, cardinal 43, winter wren 42, house wren and tufted titmouse 31, scarlet tanager and marsh wren 30 and yellowthroat 29.

As I suggested earlier, it is easy to question Hartshorne's assignments. Consider just one example. He assigns a 48 to the superb lyrebird of Australia but the 9s that this bird earns for loudness and imitativeness in no way reflect a fair comparison with other species. Tim Holt in his book about

Australian birds, *Where Song Began*, tells us, "A lyrebird's song can reportedly reach a hillside 3 kilometers [2 miles] away; up close, it hurts the human ear." And Holt's list of this species' imitations includes: in addition to dozens of bird songs, the wing beats of pigeons, the howling of dogs, swans honking, young magpies begging, a smoker's hack, ambulance sirens; koalas grunting, parrots rustling their feathers. Pet lyrebirds imitate rattling chains, violins, pianos, saws, garbled human conversation with an occasional "Hey Bill" thrown in, and the cries of children. These are off the chart in comparison with other birds and thus underrepresent this species' singing quality. Our mockingbird has a remarkable repertoire of imitations but ornithologists who have listened to both it and the lyrebird agree that there is no comparison. Hartshorne himself later referred to the lyrebird as a Shakespeare among birds, ranking it first among 194 superior singers.

We can, of course, still make up our own minds about our personal best singer.

I once spent an afternoon with Paul Kellogg, the engineer who initiated the Cornell Laboratory's collection of sounds. We listened to the songs of winter wrens and hermit thrushes first at full speed and then at reduced speeds. Each time the speed was halved the key dropped an octave until we were listening to baritone and bass notes. For me that afternoon forever determined my choice for best singer among the birds I know: a tie between that tinkling wren song and the organ tones of the hermit thrush. I miss my visits to northern forests where I could listen to their songs, especially at dawn and in the evening.

22. Rediscovery of a Missing Bird

You may recall how excited ornithologists were in 2004 when evidence suggested that an ivory-billed woodpecker, a species believed to have been extinct for sixty years, was found in Arkansas. Note that, despite much effort including the use of electronic equipment designed to record the woodpeckers' calls, no widely accepted confirming evidence has been produced since the initial report.

That sixty years is dwarfed by an earlier return from what was believed to have been extinction, a story well told by Buffalonian Elizabeth Gehrman in her new book, *Rare Birds*. Here is a precis of her story.

The Bermuda petrel or cahow (pronounced CA-how with the a sounding like the a in mash) was so common when sailors first approached Bermuda in the 16th century that the volume of their cries gave the island its early name, Devil's Isle. Estimates number the birds in the millions.

Unfortunately, those early visits also began the demise of these birds. By the mid-1500s pigs had been introduced to the island. This was standard procedure for sailors: the pigs would breed and be available for harvest when their ships passed that way again. With less purpose, cats, dogs, goats and especially rats were also introduced. As if those scavengers weren't enough threat to the birds, humans arrived in 1609, the first a group of castaways. As one report had it, they proceeded to "take, kill, roaste and eate" the petrels. Another report tells us, "We dried and salted more than a thousand. The men ate them all the time, and they were so plentiful that four thousand could be killed at the same spot in a single night."

The result: the last report of the cahow was in 1612 and it was believed to be extinct by about 1625. Like the dodo and the passenger pigeon the world had apparently lost another species.

But then in 1951 after a lapse of almost 400 years the birds were rediscovered by a team led by the famous American ornithologist Robert Cushman Murphy. (Only in 1993 were the first cahows seen at sea.)

Why then were they not found for so long?

The life history of the cahow addresses that question. This species spends its first five years wandering at sea, rarely even resting on the water and probably even sleeping in flight. Only after that long period do the adults return each year briefly to their home site to breed. Their noisy courtship takes place during the darkest nights. Once the female is inseminated, the pair departs once again to allow the female's single egg to mature in her body.

When the time comes for delivery, the pair, bonded for life, returns to nest in an underground cavity. The egg is laid and incubated alternately by the parents until it hatches to produce a chick that requires only a few more days before it is ready to fly. Then the parents simply leave, the chick climbs out of the nest into the light and after a few attempts flies off to continue that cycle of life. Thus we have rare visits to underground nesting sites on tiny rock outcroppings that are difficult for humans to explore, all this combined with only nighttime activities by the petrels. It was for these reasons that this species went so long unrecorded.

But there were hints that the birds were around. Gehrman describes how inhabitants of small islands in the Bermudan archipelago and Portuguese fishermen were familiar with the cahows, but in Bermuda's highly stratified society, these people were considered second-class citizens and their observations went unrecorded.

Shortly before the 1951 discovery, Fred Hall, then a Coast Artillery captain but later director of the Buffalo Museum of Science, played a small role in this story. He heard "cries from the outer islands" and found other evidence of the birds' presence but, although he shared this information with his ornithological colleagues, he failed to publish his observations.

In Gehrman's lively story, David Wingate shares center stage with the Bermuda petrel. As a 15-year old, Wingate was with Murphy when the bird was rediscovered and he devoted his life to its protection. It is estimated that there are now about 250 cahows breeding in Bermuda largely due to his efforts.

23. Big Noses

It's early September and we are spending two days on Long Island counting big noses — more accurately gull-sized birds with big beaks — that are rare on the Niagara Frontier.

Our hosts, Tom and Diana Killip, take us on a tour of the barrier beaches from Jamaica Bay to Montauk Point, but most of our time is spent near the Atlantic Ocean outlet of Shinnecock Bay.

Our first big nose, the American oystercatcher, is an awkward appearing shorebird with a heavy plover-like shape. It has an overall black and white appearance, the black head color extending to the throat as well leaving only the belly white. It stands on heavy gray legs. More prominently it also has a thick orange bill fully twice as long as the rest of its head.

To me the appearance of this bird places it somewhere between silly and ugly. But what does it care? To another oystercatcher I am certain that it is a handsome specimen. And the massive bill is important. As the tide retreats, clams are exposed in the sand. When one of these bivalves relaxes its shell to take its first (and last) breath of air, the oystercatcher steps up and, its bill serving its role perfectly, neatly slices the tendon that holds the two shells so firmly together. A few quick scoops and the oystercatcher has eaten the exposed delicacy. No shore restaurant serves fresher blue points.

The second of our big noses is the black skimmer. A dozen of these slim tern-like birds with black backs, white throat and belly, and short red legs stand close together on an exposed sand bar facing into the wind. So far not very unusual, but now add to each bird a heavy, bright red, black-tipped bill even thicker than the oystercatcher's and as long as the bird's head and neck together. The lower mandible is bigger and a full inch longer than the upper. This bird has (switching metaphors) the strongest under-bite since King Kong. It stands with body horizontal, appearing weighted down with this outsized beak.

But now one skimmer takes off on wings spanning four feet. It quarters over the only inches-deep tidal waters. Sailing rapidly and under the perfect control of these powerful wings, it tips forward and plows the end of that lower bill along the unruffled, soft blue surface of the bay, leaving a tiny motorboat-like wake. Every fifteen to twenty yards it scoops up a minnow and with a well-practiced head motion neatly aligns it to be swallowed. The water is so smooth that, when the bird's bill is raised from the water to do this, we see an inverted bird reflected below. Now when it reinserts its bill into the water the skimmer and its reflection appear to kiss.

All of the awkward appearance of the standing birds is gone and we have a beautiful black, white, and red bird in perfect harmony with its environment. Standing, it was Jimmy Durante; in flight it is Kevin Costner.

Our third big nose is more a Pinocchio than the others, for the even longer bill of the marbled godwit is at least slim. If we extend the Pinocchio analogy, the godwit must be one of the most spectacular liars of the bird world.

It is another shorebird, appearing still chubbier than the oystercatcher. Unlike the others, this bird is brown, in appearance like a larger, longer-billed yellowlegs. The bill is slightly upturned and well over twice the length of its head. One of the two we see conveniently raises its wings to show distinguishing cinnamon linings.

In the evening away from the shore we even find a fourth big nose, the smaller American woodcock. Unlike the others this is a woodland bird, its long bill with a flexible tip that allows it to probe deeply into the forest floor for insects and worms.

24. Exotics

Bill Eaton's home and next door antique shop are on lower Elmwood Avenue, but his backyard is a tiny park in the heart of Buffalo. Surrounding his small in-ground swimming pool are a number of twenty to thirty-foot evergreens.

When I arrived last week in answer to his phoned invitation, Bill took me to a kitchen window opening onto this yard. He then went outside and spread several scoops of bird seed on the tile surface beside the pool.

Before he even reentered the kitchen, house sparrows flew down from his trees and, as the word spread, from farther away until almost a hundred milled about pecking at the seeds.

I was surprised to see no house finches, our more recent immigrant, among the sparrows. Bill told me that he occasionally sees them, but it was clear that those blusterers had not been able to intimidate this large group of house sparrows the way they have at many suburban feeders.

But now joining the drab brown and black sparrows appeared a fashion plate, a slim, pastel blue bird. It was a parakeet — or more technically a budgerigar. And within a minute or two a second parakeet joined it, this one blue-green. Slighter and more wary than the sparrows, these miniature parrots still fed among them in close proximity.

Bill had called me to ask how he might capture these exotic birds. He feels — as I do — that they will not survive the harsher weather ahead. I referred him to Art Clark at the museum, who suggested that he bait a cage. Bill is in the process of borrowing a cage to do this. And he has posted notices urging the owner who has lost these birds to reclaim them.

Although a parakeet appearing at a local feeder is unusual — and two is even more remarkable — such an event is not unique. Bill Burch told me about another 'budgie' that came to the Lenehan's feeder on Grand Island last year from May until at least December. That bird also associated with house sparrows.

Budgerigars, originally from Australia, have now established wild breeding populations in southern Florida and for that reason are counted (only when seen in that area) by bird listers. Among other parrots established in Florida, the much larger monk parakeet, has also made brief inroads into New York State. Unlike the budgerigars, however, this species poses a significant threat. In South America troops of monk parakeets do much agricultural damage, especially to fruit crops. To head off similar problems here, the bulky nests of the few escaped birds in this state are destroyed.

These observations remind me of a note I received last April from Carol Hildebrand of Newfane. At her feeder another foreign visitor, a European goldfinch, had appeared. This species is easily distinguishable from American goldfinches by the bright red patch on the front of the face, this red accented by surrounding crescents of white and black. The yellow in this bird's wing is also located in a different area from that of our goldfinch in winter plumage.

"He appeared to be very hungry and quite aggressive," said Mrs. Hildebrand. "He wouldn't share the feeder with the other finches."

Although I visited the Hildebrand yard, I was unable to find this bird. But in January 1990, I had seen one of these lovely finches at the Ronan's feeder in Arcade.

For a time several decades ago a small group of European goldfinches nested on Long Island. It is said that these birds were released by an illegal importer when authorities raided his New York City shop. The species still breeds regularly in the Bahamas. But the ones observed here, like the parakeets, are almost certainly escaped cage birds.

25. Below the Falls

My behavior didn't strike me as especially odd, but you may disagree.

I am talking about my only ride on "The Maid of the Mist" through the rapids just below Niagara Falls. I was with my son and daughter-in-law who were visiting from Denver, each of us sweating in those lead-weighted yellow slickers.

As the boat chugged toward the base of Horseshoe Falls, the attention of everyone on board was riveted on the cascade of water falling closer and closer. Everyone except me, that is. I was turned away watching a few gulls that were as inattentive to the nearby falls as I was.

They were not the gulls that we see more and more often away from the lakes at each end of this Niagara River, Lake Erie to the south, Ontario to the north. Especially when storms threaten or fields are plowed, ring-billed and herring gulls congregate inland. And they have discovered fast food too. Near any restaurant dumpster you are almost certain to find a few. Already many local youngsters think that the MacDonald's trademark is two arches with a gull standing on one of them.

These gulls below the falls were smaller, less than half as bulky as even ring-billed gulls. When they rested on the water, they were also more buoyant than the bigger birds, sitting head erect, bodies riding high in the waves. And their erratic flight pattern made them seem still lighter. Darting first one way then another, only occasionally dipping to the water to pick up a minnow, they seemed to have no care in the world.

These were Bonaparte's gulls, a special favorite of mine. This species is commonly seen along the Niagara River during spring and fall migrations.

I was reminded of this experience when I went to Squaw Island, later renamed Unity Island, to try to locate a rare Sabine's gull that had been reported there. I found no Sabine's but did see dozens of these Bonaparte's gulls patrolling up and down the river together with some equally graceful common terns. The number of these gulls will increase through the fall until harsher winter weather will drive them southwest through Lake Erie.

Because of their similarities and many plumages, gulls present identification problems. Like most others, the Bonaparte's body color is white, its back light gray, and its wing tips black. In breeding plumage adults have striking black heads, but even this is not diagnostic. Other less common gulls like the Franklin's, little, black-headed, Sabine's, and laughing gulls share this black hood. But at this time of year few of these birds retain the hood anyway. Instead their heads are all mostly white, the Bonaparte's, little, and black-headed gulls with a black dot behind the eye.

Especially in flight, the adult and immature "Boneys," as birders call them, appear quite different. Many first-time observers think that they are seeing two distinct species. The adult appears very light with a distinguishing white leading edge to its gray-mantled wings. The immature birds are just as handsome but their wings are outlined in black and the tips of their tails are black as well.

French Emperor Napoleon I had a nephew named Charles Lucien Bonaparte. Unlike other members of this family whose energies turned to government and warfare, Charles chose a career in science. When he was in his early twenties, he moved to a home near Philadelphia, where, beginning in 1825, he published four volumes supplementing Alexander Wilson's *American Ornithology*. Despite his brief five years here, Charles Lucien Bonaparte has been called "the father of systematic ornithology in this country." His name is memorialized in that of this lovely little gull.

Look for Bonaparte's gulls from the boatyards, the fishing piers, and the scenic overlooks along the Niagara River. This species should at least partially restore your appreciation for this opportunistic bird family.

26. Feeding Birds

Anyone can gain pleasure from feeding birds. As I have described, when she was in a nursing home, my mother placed a few crumbs on an outside windowsill to attract sparrows and pigeons, their visits giving her hours of simple pleasure. My wife, also not a birder, speaks of "her" cardinal family, the "husband" escorting and sometimes feeding "his wife" beneath our feeder where chickadees and house finches have dropped seeds. (Joining in this anthropomorphizing, I have visions of a kingbird having conferred the blessings of ornithological matrimony on these two.)

Feeding can range from a few corncobs thrown on a patio deck or table to expensive triple plastic and metal towers containing specialized foods, some, like Niger seed, imported from foreign countries.

If you wish to begin feeding birds, my advice is to start simple. Don't buy expensive feeders that squirrels and raccoons will quickly destroy, in the process destroying your willingness to try again. Instead merely put out in an exposed place a seed mix that includes sunflower seeds. Or hang from a tree limb a small slab of butcher's suet in a string onion bag. Then be prepared for days or even weeks before birds discover your bounty, and for an initial concentration of house sparrows at the seed and starlings at the suet.

But if you prevail you will find more and more interesting birds visiting your food source. Often the first among these will be house finches, the sparrow-sized males with a rosy background to their brown streaks. Then sooner or later will come chickadees and jays and nuthatches and cardinals and juncos and mourning doves and less common birds until your interest is captured for all time.

My wife and I have several times graduated from simple feeders to the complex products of local garden stores, but each time we have been punished. Inevitably squirrels have gotten to those better feeders, knocking them down, chewing through the plastic, and making them useless. We now are back to a small satellite feeder mounted close under an inverted bowl, the strong nylon string that holds it tied to a high tree limb. It hangs about six feet off the ground, well away from the trunk of the supporting tree. Squirrels cannot jump to it from below and those that try to leap or slide to it from above are fended off by the bowl. Nearby a rubberized metal suet feeder is similarly mounted.

One problem with suet is that it turns rancid. Here is a recipe for a suet substitute that avoids this problem, passed on to me by Mike Galas. You will need ingredients in these portions: 5 pounds of cornmeal, 1 2/3 pounds of flour, 1 pound of ground egg shells, 2 pounds of peanut hearts, 1 pound of raisins, and 4 pounds of lard.

Local feed stores carry the dry materials except for eggshells. To include them you'll have to collect and grind the eggshells yourself. It is possible to omit them, but grit is important to birds. They have no teeth and an abrasive in their craw is necessary for them to digest food. That is one of the things birds are after when you see them feeding along roadsides in winter.

Mix the dry ingredients in a large container. Melt and add the lard, blending evenly. Shape the mixture into suet balls, spoon it into forms that fit your feeders, or smear it on pine cones to be hung like ornaments from tree limbs. Refrigerate in baggies what you don't use immediately.

Locate your feeders where you can observe them from a kitchen, living room or study window. If you do this, you'll soon join the many thousands who derive great pleasure from their close and supportive encounters with their feathered neighbors.

27. Boreal Owl

A rare boreal owl was spotted in Rock Point Provincial Park in nearby Canada just a week before one visited western New York. I joined dozens of Canadian and United States birders looking unsuccessfully for this little owl the next day after it was reported. We did find among the pines and spruces that decorate this park three long-eared owls, a gray phase screech owl, and a saw-whet owl. Several observers also found a snowy owl just west of the park at Lowbanks, but the boreal owl was not relocated. Non-birders would have found it strange to see people going from evergreen to evergreen, pushing aside branches and scanning the exposed trees from top to bottom. They might have guessed that these folks were searching for pine cones and they would not have been far wrong: the boreal owl, at nine to ten inches, is the same size as the largest white pine cones.

But birders were not alone in searching the trees and brambles. A Cooper's hawk that had been patrolling the lakeshore suddenly dove into a thicket and carried off a robin-sized prey. This episode may have represented the demise of the owl we were seeking.

To the ancient Greeks Boreas was the god of the north wind and boreal is derived from this name. Biologists refer to the region of coniferous forests that circle the Northern Hemisphere as the boreal zone and this is exactly home territory for the boreal owl. Across Canada this region extends from the northernmost east-west highways and railroads to the barren muskeg of the still farther north.

There are only about a dozen records of the boreal owl for New York State. Local birders who want a chance to see it and another rare species of the far north, the great gray owl, usually travel in the dead of winter to Amherst Island near Kingston, Ontario.

What then was this owl doing here? That question is a difficult one to answer. One guess is that its appearance presages an eruption of northern species into this area this winter. The early appearance of several snowy owls, pine siskins and evening grosbeaks here and some redpolls and bohemian waxwings near Toronto support this possibility.

Some believe that these periodic southward migrations of northern species are caused by poor food crops in their home territory: a bad year for pine cones, for example. More recently biologists have suggested that the opposite is the cause. A series of several years of good crops and mild weather leads to breeding success and inevitably overpopulation. Then even the good food supply is not enough and some birds are forced to join this seasonal emigration.

Whatever the cause of these incursions, they provide extra excitement for birders, who will be on the lookout for these northern visitors in the winter months ahead.

28. Reestablishing a Raptor

The bird flapped steadily toward us from far down Kioskokwi Lake. As we watched its approach through binoculars, it seemed to grow in size. I found myself going through a series of identification trials based on this growth: crow, raven, red-tailed hawk and finally eagle.

It was indeed an eagle: a fish eagle or osprey. Soon we could make out its dark forward thrusting shoulders and, when it finally reached our end of the lake and sailed above us, we could easily see the white body and head markings.

Now the osprey put on a show. It soared directly over our canoe perhaps a hundred feet above us, so close in my glasses that I could see it tip its head and look down at us with an intense yellow eye. A few yards on it suddenly veered into a stall, did a wingover and plummeted straight down, hitting the water with a tremendous splash just yards away.

That act was so close, abrupt and unexpected that I felt for a moment that the bird had dived at us and missed. It was soon apparent that this was wrong for the osprey now rose from the water, awkwardly and straining at first, but soon regaining its graceful flight. In one fist it carried a big lake trout.

It flew a few hundred yards back down the lake to a tall white pine. There we could see it land on a big stick nest partially hidden in the green foliage.

When this unforgettable experience happened in Algonquin Park in about 1970, it had a somber aspect. We thought that we might be seeing one of the last of this species. Pesticide residues had been accumulating up the food chain from water plants through aquatic worms and insects, crustaceans and amphibians, fish and finally to this beautiful bird. As a result almost all osprey eggs were then either sterile or had such thin shells that the adults broke them while brooding. We looked hopefully, but we could see no young on the nest in the pine.

Fortunately the publication of Rachel Carson's *Silent Spring* in 1962 contributed to the demise of DDT a decade later and to subsequent tighter limitations on some of the other pesticides with long-term toxicity. Those restrictions saved the osprey.

To encourage them to relocate in western New York, in the 1990s osprey chicks were brought from Long Island to the Oak Orchard Wildlife Refuge where they were hacked — that is, raised with as little human contact as possible. It was several years before the results of those releases were evident, because young ospreys first migrate to Central and South America and do not re-cross our southern border for 16 months. But the results are clear today.

As evidence of its recovery, Buffalo Ornithological Society May and October censuses show migrating osprey numbers double from their low in the 1960s to the 1980s, double again in the 1990s and a steady increase ever since. There are enough ospreys in this region now that they create a problem for telephone companies. To avoid their nesting on the wires around the tops of telephone poles where they can disrupt service, platforms have been added and you can now see osprey nests on those platforms near many of our lakes and streams.

29. Winter Finches

Some years are unusual for people who feed wild birds. Winter finches, some of them rarely recorded here, crowd their feeding stations.

In late 1993, for example, Yves Cormier, a Nova Scotia birder, reported an early and heavy migration through his region of pine and evening grosbeaks and common redpolls as well as snowy owls, black-backed woodpeckers, boreal chickadees, Bohemian waxwings, Northern shrikes and snow buntings. Many pine siskins then appeared through New England and as far west as Albany. Evening grosbeaks reached New Jersey, Ohio, Ithaca, New York and Pennsylvania. Purple finches increased in numbers in Massachusetts until they even outnumbered house finches at some feeders. And a massive movement of red-breasted nuthatches was recorded in the Midwest and along the Atlantic coast.

Those years are indeed rare but it is reasonable to prepare for them.

How can you identify new finches at your feeders? Here are some suggestions. (Note that birders often stretch the definition of winter finches to include species like those of Cormier's list that depart far from the Fringillid family; here I will restrict myself to true finches.)

First, of course, you should get to know well the common finches of your feeders: goldfinch and house finch. Accustom yourself to the drab brown and gray winter colors that replace the bright yellows of goldfinches and to the color variations in house finches that range from simple brown streaking to orange and red and occasionally even yellow feathering.

Now consider the less common finches.

First, evening grosbeak. If outsize "goldfinches" with especially big strong bills appear at your feeder, this is your species. The first few always create great excitement, but that excitement will soon pale. They are seed store favorites as they rapidly consume bushels of sunflower seeds. (Formerly a rather common winter visitor to this region, evening grosbeak numbers have suffered a serious decline and are now included on the watch list of the 2016 *State of North America's Birds*.)

That is an easy identification. The rest are harder.

Delicately striped brown birds that often consort with goldfinches are pine siskins. They show small and varying amounts of yellow in their wings, at the base of their tail and sometimes in their throat. Their smaller size will distinguish them from house finches. They are also identifiable by the extended buzzy *shreeee* of their calls.

Common redpolls also have brown striping on their bodies, but they are easily recognized by the bright red bellhop cap perched on their forehead. The hoary redpoll, an even rarer visitor, has less streaking and, as its name implies, appears much whiter.

Remember that goldfinches, siskins and redpolls are all about the same small size.

Purple finches must be separated from the more plentiful house finches. The color of the male purple finch is more rose red than purple and it is not easy to distinguish this species by color alone. Unlike the male house finch, however, the male purple finch's red runs down its back to its rump. Both purple and house finch females are striped brown birds but the female purple finch has a contrasting brown cheek patch and white eyeline.

Crossbills seldom come to feeders. If you are lucky enough to have them visit yours, you'll know them by the strange adaptation to feeding on pine cones identified by the name, crossbill: their upper and lower mandibles overlap like an X. These birds are slightly larger than house finches and evident wing-bars easily separate the white-winged and red species.

Among the handsomest of all birds is the pine grosbeak. Robin sized, plump and stocky, males are tinged with pink, females with yellow. These rare but remarkably tame visitors might come to your feeder for sunflower seeds; more often you would see a flock feeding on fruit buds in an orchard or among the red candles of staghorn sumacs.

So get your hoppers filled with sunflower seed, stuff your feeding tubes with niger thistle grain and hang out your suet bags. This could be THE winter.

30. Banders

A few years ago I spent a very pleasant Saturday at the Beaver Meadow Audubon Center in North Java, attending an informal meeting of the bird banders of Western New York and northern Pennsylvania. Dave Junkin, then center director-naturalist and a bander himself, convened that annual get-together.

It has been almost seventy years since I gave up my own banding permit, but I still found myself comparing my experiences with those of the enthusiastic men and women at this meeting.

I trapped only a few dozen birds each year: most of these banders trap hundreds, and a few even thousands annually. I used only two traps for ground feeders and that kind of trap today is only a minor tool in the bander's arsenal. Now, for example, they string many yards of mist netting across flight lanes, the nets serving like giant spider webs to capture flying birds, And now they even capture hawks and owls with rodent or pigeon-baited cages.

Jerry Farrell of Lewiston described how he uses these raptor traps. Inside the hardware cloth cage he places a purchased pet-store mouse. He then drives into rural Niagara County and, when he sees a hawk, drops his trap at the side of the road. "Even if the hawk is a quarter mile away," he says, "its extraordinary vision immediately picks out the rodent and it heads in." When the hawk lights on the cage, its talons are caught in fish line loops, and it is quickly captured, unhooked, banded and released. "While all this is happening." said Farrell, "the tame mouse simply sits in the cage preening. It has no idea how threatened it was."

Each of these banders contributes in a significant way to our understanding of bird populations and migration. A few of the numbered metal rings they attach to the birds' legs are identified by other banders or people who find dead birds. When this information is returned to the U. S. Fish & Wildlife

Service in Washington, both finder and bander are notified of the other's location.

Some of the time at Saturday's meeting was spent sharing the locations of these "foreign re-traps:" places like Winnipeg and Manitoba in Canada and Charleston, West Virginia. While this discussion was going on, my mind turned to an old story told by Frederick Lincoln, who once headed the federal banding program.

Early in the history of United States bird banding, it seems, the bands were distributed by the Bureau of Biological Survey, predecessor of the Fish & Wildlife Service. An early order for bands placed in England asked for the abbreviated return address label: "Wash., D.C. Biol. Surv." The entire shipment of bands came back with this text creatively revised to read: "Wash, Boil, Serve."

There are many other aspects of banding. Age information is collected by re-trapping. For example. Betsy Brooks, who heads the team of banders at Braddock Bay near Rochester and also bands at her home in Alfred Station, has recorded the same pair of yellow warblers in each of eight consecutive years. This is a remarkable longevity record for these delicate songsters whose average life span is less than a year. Banders also record bird weights, abnormalities, injuries and the parasites that infest their feathers.

Even more important, banding stations are often visited by schoolchildren whose experiences touching beautiful songbirds give them lasting positive attitudes toward wildlife.

Banders contribute their time and pay for their equipment. Even becoming licensed is increasingly difficult, and they must submit detailed reports. But as Don Clark of Farmersville Station said "Each time I hold a bluebird in my hand, I am fully rewarded for all my time and effort."

31. Early April

After a nasty winter that carried on far too long making early spring dismal as well, it is finally time to respond to my friend Barbara's request for some good news for a change.

Good news indeed. One thing about climbing out of a winter like that: it makes late April and early May a wonderful time here on the Niagara Frontier.

Glorious days ahead: the two dozen species of warblers are coming. And these colorful little migrants will bring with them vireos, sparrows and flycatchers; thrushes, wrens and buntings; tanagers, orioles and bobolinks; about a hundred species of our summer birds of neighborhood and forest.

Even if the weather stays cold and dreary (snowflakes are in the air as I write) the inherited pressure to migrate will bring back those birds.

Already the woods are full of golden-crowned kinglets and brown creepers, their high-pitched voices now beyond my hearing range. In another week ruby-crowned kinglets will begin to replace the golden-crowned and their bubbling calls will lead us to flocks of these small birds. If you are fortunate you will sometimes find another member of this clan: the blue-gray gnatcatcher. They too are an early migrant but are far less common than the kinglets and chickadees and titmice they occasionally join.

Tree swallows are already here and the other swallows and purple martin will soon follow. And the woods are filling with yellow-bellied sapsuckers, those specialized woodpeckers that drill a ring of holes around a tree trunk and return later to savor the sap draining from them. In May hummingbirds will also feed at those sap sources.

You have to look with care to find our earliest brown thrush: the hermit thrush. Peak migration for those other brown thrushes — Swainson's, gray-cheeked and wood thrushes and veery — won't occur until early May. When you do catch sight of a hermit thrush, usually on the ground, it is best identified by its reddish tail. Unfortunately, this species rarely sings in this region as its beautiful organ-like song is one of the real treats offered by our northern forests.

But the winter wren does sing here occasionally during migration. Listen for its lovely notes. The volume and number of those notes are remarkable, especially coming from another of our tiniest birds. Soon the more monotonous chatter of the house wren will be heard more often. Its noisy calls will continue through the summer whereas the winter wren will move farther north or into deeper forests.

Listen now in open fields for the whistles of meadowlarks, the buzzing song of the savannah sparrow, the increasing tempo of the field sparrow's *dee*-ing, from high overhead the *hoohoohoo*… sound made by snipe wings but only later the chattering of bobolinks.

Two warblers have already arrived. Pine warblers are piping from the top of evergreens, their songs difficult for me to differentiate not only from chipping sparrows but from juncos as well. And all three are to be found in similar locales. The other early warbler migrant is the Louisiana waterthrush. To find them you must usually visit deeply shaded shale-sided glens. But these species will soon be followed by troops of yellow-rumped warblers with a few palm warblers mixed in.

Yes, there are many species here already, but the real gang will arrive in the coming weeks.

Years ago as a beginning birder I wondered when was the most exciting time for this activity. To respond to that question I derived from the records of the Genesee Ornithological Society in Rochester information that provided the basis for a paper I wrote titled, "The Pattern of Bird Arrival." (Like many of my other papers it was never published.) In it I sought to identify the most exciting time of year for bird watchers. The key feature of my presentation was a graph indicating the number of species to be found in that area week by week through the year. I used the slope of

that graph to represent "bird arrival" and the steepest slope —
which I defined as that most exciting time — occurred during
the last weeks of April and the first few days of May. So we
can now look forward to exactly that time: the best for bird
watching.

Some of you readers are thinking: those birds may be
returning but I never see them. Others among you cannot
identify the ones you do see. A suggestion to both groups: go
on any morning in the next two weeks when it is not raining
to a local haven for bird watchers — for us, Mirror Lake at
Forest Lawn Cemetery or Tifft Nature Preserve — and you
should find experienced birders who will be happy to point
out some of these colorful species. You just have to ask what
they are seeing.

32. Hawk Watch

Running just inside the east entrance of Lakeside Memorial Park in Hamburg, New York, a jogger passed a line of parked cars and a group of people sitting on lawn chairs looking up at the sky with binoculars. He slowed to a stop and asked pleasantly, "What are you folks doing?"

One of the observers responded, "We're looking at hawks."

The runner peered up briefly and, seeing nothing but blue sky and clouds, shook his head and jogged on. I am certain that he thought that he had been caught by the old "Look! Look!" trick.

But as the jogger trotted down the road into the park, I was looking at a kettle of almost fifty hawks. Kettle is the term hawk watchers have adopted for such a group of hawks. The name was chosen because the hawks appear like those tiny bubbles that move about in a seething pot just before it comes to a boil.

Even with my binoculars some of the hawks were tiny specks in the sky, perhaps a half-mile distant. Some flew in line, others in slow circles, but all moved northeast toward the eastern end of Lake Erie. There a few would swing to the west and would soon pass another hawk watching station at Grimsby, Ontario; others would continue northeast and would be seen by hawk watchers at Braddock's Bay near Rochester and farther east at Oswego's Sandy Ponds lookout. Most would then continue north to spend the summer in the vast forests of the Adirondacks and Canada.

It was a remarkable experience to have so many hawks in one binocular field. At that great distance the tiny dots appeared like those no-see-ums that circle in front of your eyes in spring and summer woodlots. After I looked down to rest my neck, I found it difficult to find them again.

With the birds that far away, it took an expert like Jim Landau to point out species to me. Jim regularly reports the numbers of migrating raptors passing this location to the Hawk Migration Association of North America. On this day most were broad-winged hawks, less than half the size of our resident red-tails. But soaring with the broad-wings on this early May morning were a few ospreys, those almost eagle-sized fish hawks, as well as turkey vultures, sharp-shinned hawks, and kestrels. Nearer to us two Cooper's hawks that reside in the park woods flew with graceful wing beats, courting in slow circles part way up to the migrants.

Over time rarer birds are seen from this vantage point as well. On some years both bald and golden eagles are recorded here as are goshawks, those fierce symbols of the wild north country. Falcons are represented as well by merlins and peregrines. And black vultures are beginning to wander north.

Where we sat we could feel the wind blowing from the north off Lake Erie. This would seem to oppose this flight; instead the light breeze contributed to the lift that helped the raptors soar.

To see why, you need only recall from junior high school science three weather effects: (1) dry land changes temperature faster than water, (2) cold air flows toward warm, and (3) warmer air rises. On this sunny spring day, the lake remained much colder than the land to its south and the air cooled by the lake flowed inland toward the air heated by the land, thus creating the breeze we felt. This onshore breeze drove a wedge under the warmer air, forcing that air upward in what are called thermals. It was that rising air that provided the lift for the migrating hawks.

In exactly the way hawks do, glider pilots utilize such thermals to maintain altitude or even to rise to higher levels. In fact glider pilots often take cues from nearby soaring hawks.

On that day there was very little wind so the birds had to fly thousands of feet above us to take advantage of the thermals. If there had been a wind out of the south of perhaps five to ten miles per hour, what I have described would have taken effect at a much lower level and we would have been able to watch the birds just a few hundred feet overhead.

Even the jogger would have seen them then.

33. Pete Dunn

Some years ago Pete Dunn spoke at the Buffalo Museum of Science. His title for that year's annual William C. Vaughan Memorial Lecture was "The Feather Quest."

I had heard Dunn in Watertown the previous year at the Federation of New York State Bird Clubs meeting. His talk there was perfect. He told a story that was as attractive to backyard bird watchers as it was to serious ornithologists. It had both history and fantasy; it had technical birding but it told of the practical problems all outdoor adventurers face. All this was supported by an underlying cast of droll humor.

Dunn's book of the same title, *The Feather Quest*, is the story of a year Pete and his wife Linda spent traveling North America looking for birds.

I don't usually cotton to such books. Years ago I read "Wild America" by Roger Tory Peterson and James Fisher about a similar year-long trip across the continent. It left me thinking only how impossible such an expedition would be. Even then a few hours of birding was enough for me; after that my concentration waned, my energy flagged.

I was left with no such feeling reading *The Feather Quest*. It conveys a very different quality. A number of frantic days are described, including the record run of their team accumulating 210 species to win the annual World Series of Birding in New Jersey. But the focus here is broader and includes interesting people as well as remarkable birds, quiet times as well as reckless chases, evocative portrayals of beautiful scenery as well as clarifying descriptions of colorful plumage.

This is the book for those who don't understand the sport of birding, something that is different from but not opposed to the study of birds as individuals. Listen to Dunn start his year list: "In birding, as in the spirit of New Year's, January first makes all things new again. All the birds tallied last year went the way of the old year at midnight. This morning Linda and I faced a clean slate and all birds, no matter how common, no matter how often they may have engaged our lives, became new again, became 'Year Birds' as the expression goes. It's just a game, of course, one of many, and it keeps birding fun."

Later he speaks of another aspect of this sport: "Looking at birds is a little like viewing art in a gallery. The difference is that birding adds an element of excitement that galleries lack, the excitement born of risk. Wild birds are free and we see them at their sufferance — or we may not see them at all. That's the risk. That's the element of gain and loss that motivates human ambition."

And so the Dunns visit many of the nation's birding hotspots: the Everglades and Attu, Newburyport and the Rio Grande, nearby Point Pelee and Cape May, Hawk Mountain and the Gulf Coast, Colorado grasslands and offshore Monterey.

In passing, several birders from this area are mentioned: Kayo Roy, Harold Axtell and those wonderful displaced New Yorkers, Walter and Sally Hoyt Spofford, whose south Texas hummingbird garden was a must stop for old friends. Sadly today Axtell and the Spoffords are no longer with us.

At book and year end there is no headlong rush to accumulate the 600-and-somethingth species; instead the Dunns join a rural Kansas Christmas Count on a bitterly cold December day. "Good" birds are a ruffed grouse and a barred owl. The message is clear: Totals are ephemeral; it is the experience that counts.

Here Pete Dunn draws close to this birder's heart.

34. Owl Man

A few days after my visit to Montana the American Ornithologists' Union, the major organization of scientists who study birds, met in Missoula. One of the best opportunities that meeting offered was a session led by Denver Holt of the Owl Research Institute that is based in Missoula.

I know this because I spent a day with Holt and one of his associates, Mike Maples, in Montana. That afternoon we watched these "owl men" record information about long-eared owls and in the evening they took us to the nest of a western screech owl.

Long-eared owls are uncommon winter visitors to the Niagara Frontier and rarely remain to nest here. In Montana both pairs of owls we observed were reusing old magpie nests, big tangles of sticks in cottonwood thickets.

When we arrived Holt and Maples were setting up a mist net in an attempt to capture an adult owl. Theirs looked exactly like a badminton net, but they placed it where it would have been difficult to play that game: in a lane through the thicket the owl regularly followed flying to its nest.

Once the net was erected we moved behind a hedgerow. There we waited for the owl to return to its nest from the nearby fence post where it sat intently watching us.

Sure enough, in a few minutes it took off, ranged overhead in that erratic long-winged flight pattern common to these and short-eared owls, then suddenly dipped low to the ground to speed into the narrow lane.

Holt and Maples ran ahead and, by the time we arrived, were carefully taking the owl from the net in which it was tangled. We had a wonderful opportunity to observe this handsome bird as it calmly accepted its physical examination and banding. It was smaller than a crow, mostly dark brown, but with attractive chestnut facial disks out of which its fierce unblinking yellow eyes peered at each of us in turn.

As soon as they had finished their measurements, the owl men released their captive. Undaunted, it calmly flew off only a few yards to perch on a tree limb.

Next we visited the nest of the other pair. There the half dozen young were already out wandering around the limbs of the shrubby growth. Quite unlike their well-groomed parents, these had to be the most unkempt birds in history: they were scowling out of what looked like fluffy but dingy white bathrobes.

The call of the western screech owl Holt showed us that evening is quite unlike that of its eastern relative. Far from the whinny of our eastern species, this bird cooed an almost continuous soft *too-too-too-too....* It was calling from its nest hole forty feet up in a suburban Missoula hardwood.

Through all of these interesting experiences, these men's enthusiasm shone clear. Holt is a fount of wisdom about owls. He told us of recording the first Montana nests of barn, boreal and flammulated owls, of finding pigmy and saw-whet owls nesting in the same dead tree, of his team's Alaska research on snowy owls and of their upcoming trip to Central America.

But most interesting to me was his contradiction of the widespread belief that large owls on a territory scare off smaller owls. Big owls do prey on their smaller cousins, but Holt told of finding six species calling at the same backwoods site: the tiny pigmy, saw-whet and boreal owls, and the much larger barred, great horned and great grays.

These owl men proved to me once again that serious science can be not only a real challenge, but also marvelous fun.

35. Regional Survey

As I pulled to the side of Haight Road in the Town of Somerset, New York, a tan sedan passed going in the opposite direction. In my rearview mirror I could see it slow and finally stop about a hundred yards down the road. Then as I climbed out and started off across the roadside ditch into the bushes, I watched the driver turn his car around in a driveway and drive back to pull up behind mine.

I returned to the road to see what he wanted.

The man climbed out of his car and asked apologetically, "Please, would you tell me what you folks are doing?" Pointing at a nearby house, he continued, "I live over there and for weeks I've seen cars pull up here mornings and their drivers walk off into those bushes. I cannot imagine what is going on."

When I explained that we were surveying birds for Nature Conservancy, my questioner visibly relaxed. After I finished, he said with a sigh of relief, "Thank goodness! I'm delighted to hear your explanation and I support you 100%. I was afraid that these expeditions might even have something to do with drug trafficking."

The (non-drug trafficking) project I was working on was the Lake Ontario Migratory Songbird Study, a scientific study sponsored by Niagara Mohawk, Rochester Gas and Electric and New York State Electric and Gas. It was exceptional in terms of duration: two years; study area covered: 220 miles of shoreline; number of study sites: over 200; and number of people involved: 60 volunteers each year and over 150 cooperating landowners.

The question being studied was whether migrating birds are equally distributed through habitat at varying distances from the Lake Ontario. Evidence from the first study year suggested that many more migrants are to be found in woodlots within a half-mile of the lake than in those farther inland. The second year data added confirmation and the final results provided Nature Conservancy better insight into what land areas most need protection.

The project required much prior planning. Our supervisor, Kris Agard, had located woodlots on aerial maps, determined ownership from town records, then contacted owners to obtain their cooperation. (She told me that the landowner response was almost universally positive.) Once she identified the survey lots, Agard marked them by placing a stake where we would stand to count and "blazed" paths to the road with orange tape. Finally, she copied maps and wrote instructions for counters to follow to reach designated areas.

Then through April, May and June during those two years we volunteers from western and central New York each devoted up to a dozen mornings to the census.

On each of my assigned dates I completed five to seven counts. I parked where directed and followed the orange-flagged obstacle course as much as a half mile across fields and creeks and through brush and tangled vines to the study site. At the stake I stood for ten minutes recording each bird seen or heard. Then back to the car and on to the next spot.

Sometimes pickings were thin. On a dreary May morning at one stop I recorded only two crows and a grackle. But other times made up for them. I watched hawks migrate overhead. Colorful rose-breasted grosbeaks, goldfinches, scarlet tanagers, indigo buntings, yellow warblers and cardinals brightened many days. And occasionally I recorded unexpected birds: a white-eyed vireo, a late winter wren, a Brewster's warbler and, on my final count, an olive-sided flycatcher calling its infamous, *Hick, three beers*.

It was gratifying to add this contribution of information to what was great fun for a long-time birdwatcher.

36. Robert Andrle

Some occupations are not simply thankless but invite animosity. I know. I have held two of them: university department chairman and basketball referee.

For 51 years Dr. Robert Andrle quietly and efficiently filled another of those roles: chairman of the statistics committee of the Buffalo Ornithological Society. Over part of that time he also served for two decades in a similar capacity for the New York State Ornithological Association. The basic task of those committees is to decide whether a rare bird report is acceptable.

Now think about it. You have seen a bird, perhaps at your backyard feeder, and you are convinced that it is a scallop-winged zip-whacker. You've carefully checked the bird's characteristics against a field guide and you are absolutely certain that's what it is. You write up a report and send it in. It is not accepted.

Several reactions immediately occur to you. That guy is attacking my integrity. He is purposely embarrassing me. Who is he to make such decisions?

Never mind that the scallop-winged zip-whacker has been extinct since 1935, that its range before that was New Zealand and that it is not distinguishable in the field from a starling. What right does he have to question my call?

That example is, of course, apocryphal and even a wee bit exaggerated, but I know those feelings. I have had records turned down myself.

I have known Bob Andrle since the 1950s and my respect for him has grown over those years. He weathered time on that statistics committee very well and, although he has given up his role as statistician, he continues as the most highly regarded Niagara Frontier ornithologist.

A few years ago a second *Atlas of Breeding Birds of New York State* was published. Dr. Andrle was senior editor of the first of those atlases in 1988 and he made important but mostly behind-the-scenes contributions to the new volume. Each of those tasks involved the direction of hundreds of field workers over a period of years, as well as the analysis of their contributions and the production of the resulting text.

Dr. Andrle's other activities have included:

* Service to the Buffalo Museum of Science in various roles including curator of vertebrate zoology; assistant, associate and acting director; fellow; and research associate.

* Preparation of the materials that led to designation of the Niagara River as the first international Important Birding Area (IBA). This Audubon Society sponsored program is part of a global effort to identify and conserve areas that are vital to birds and other biodiversity. The designation also serves the local tourism industry by bringing birders to the area from all parts of the world.

* Work for over twenty years with Buffalo and Erie County politicians as well as the N.Y. Department of Environmental Conservation (DEC) on the conversion of the Lake Erie shore brownfields area known as Times Beach into a park. That project was finally completed in 2007 and now we can walk through this lovely area on a system of boardwalks.

* Preparation of additional IBA submissions for Tifft Nature Preserve and Times Beach.

* Consulting with the DEC on various problems including the botulism that year after year decimates Lake Erie waterfowl, both residents and migrants.

* Development of bird check-lists for several local parks.

* Regional publications including a 1970 supplement to Beardslee and Mitchell's *Birds of the Niagara Frontier* and *Gulls of the Niagara Frontier,* an early compilation that has contributed to the mounting interest in these species here.

* Although best known for his authoritative work with birds, Dr. Andrle has also made major contributions to the study of local dragonflies and damselflies.

In preparing this essay I read Dr. Andrle's seminal and often quoted 1967 paper, "The Horned Guan in Mexico and

Guatemala." Reading between the lines of this formal ornithological essay, I gained a feel for his tough pursuit of this strange and now increasingly rare bird through tropical forests on the steep sides of Central American volcanoes. This hiking was recently described as "incredibly strenuous."

Well into retirement now, Bob remains for me a model of what it means to be an ornithologist who contributes locally as well as nationally. I am also proud to consider myself a friend of this fine man.

37. A Bird Population Study

"For many years a wood thrush has thrilled us through the summer with its lovely organ-like song," a reader writes and she continues, "This summer we listened in vain. Are these birds dying out?"

Inquiries like this are among the most common that I receive, outnumbered only by questions about the increase in local neighborhoods of other species many call "trash birds" like crows, gulls, starlings and grackles.

Much has been said recently about the decline in numbers of many of our woodland bird species. Most bird watchers share this concern. I side with these worriers, because I seem each year to see fewer thrushes, vireos, warblers and grassland sparrows on the Niagara Frontier.

But we all tend to believe that the good old days were better and another woodlot down the road may have gained a wood thrush when this complainer's songster disappeared. Clearly we need data against which to compare our subjective evaluations.

In fact much information is available to us. Across North America there are over 1500 annual Christmas Bird Counts and in western New York the Buffalo Ornithological Society conducts bird surveys each April, May and October as well as waterfowl counts each January.

All of those counts are affected by uneven coverage, the vagaries of local weather and the focus of some observers on rarer species. Despite these concerns they provide long-term averages that warrant our attention.

Three other kinds of counts are more carefully controlled. Each June road surveys are taken by Fish & Wildlife Service volunteers. Birds are recorded for three minutes every half mile along a 25-mile route that is identically monitored year after year. Today there are almost 2000 of these routes across the United States and Canada, 18 of them in this western New York area have been regularly surveyed since 1967.

But the most carefully controlled of all such counts are the Breeding Bird Censuses and the Winter Bird Population Studies, now sponsored by the Cornell Laboratory of Ornithology. Each requires much preparatory work. The survey tract is carefully marked to create a grid and a botanical survey is recorded in order to note temporal changes in plants as well as birds. Then the area is canvassed many times each year, identified birds recorded and active nests sought out.

Elizabeth Brooks of Alfred Station and Vivian Pitzrick of Belmont have conducted these surveys for some time and, after a year of preparation, Tom Greg censused a 27-acre section of the Beaver Meadow Wildlife Center near Java.

On a pleasant summer morning I joined Tom on one of his surveys.

For two hours we struggled up and down steep slopes, through thickets and back and forth across a boggy creek. Whenever we located a bird, Tom noted it in the appropriate square on his map. Later he had to analyze the 12 maps he accumulated over the summer. I ended the day exhausted.

I have in hand a copy of Tom's detailed report. He found 32 species on territory. Most common were veery, junco, yellowthroat, red-eyed vireo and chickadee. Five active nests were found, but every single one was parasitized by cowbirds.

During the mid-1950s an adjacent area was surveyed for three years. When Tom set out his tract most earlier section marks had disappeared so he had to start over. The areas only overlap slightly, but even so the census results provide interesting comparisons.

Birds lost: red-shouldered hawk; black-billed cuckoo; horned owl; catbird; yellow, chestnut-sided and mourning warblers; redstart; towhee; field and song sparrows. Birds gained: sharp-shinned hawk, sapsucker, pileated woodpecker, crow, nuthatches, creeper, solitary vireo, yellow-rumped warbler, swamp sparrow, junco and cowbird.

Numbers and species each increased about 20 percent, statistics that differ strikingly from national data showing annual reductions of 1 to 2 percent.

But wood thrushes? In 1954 seven caroled, in 1994 only one. This certainly supports my correspondent's concern.

38. Lake Watch

The Village of Barker's Bicentennial Park is on Lake Ontario at the north end of Quaker Road. It is only about a half-acre of lawn with attractive trees: mostly maples, a few spruce and locust, and one big catalpa. Down a ten-foot bank are two cement piers that extend a few yards out into the lake.

One morning in late October I spent two hours there watching for a brant flight.

Brant are small geese, scarcely bigger than mallards, with the general appearance of miniature Canada geese. Like Canadas their backs are dark gray, their necks and heads black, and their sides dingy white. But there the similarity ends. Instead of that white cheek of the Canada goose, a brant has only a few white marks on the neck that look a little like a bow tie. When brant fly, white tails behind dark wings and necks are good field marks.

Brant — the English call them brent — are sea geese. Most migrate from their Hudson's Bay breeding grounds through the Gulf of St. Lawrence to wintering areas along the Atlantic coast. But many years a few hundred are observed passing through the Great Lakes at this time. This was not a species new to me but I hoped on this morning to catch one of those flights.

When I arrived at dawn the broad lake appeared sterile. The blue-gray surface was corrugated by small waves and these were gathered into larger swells. Only slight cirrus clouds and a few jet contrails marked the blue sky, but the horizon was lost in fog. Through binoculars I could see a mirage of waves leaping from the surface into the mist where I would normally have seen Toronto skyscrapers.

Although the lake seemed lifeless, I set up a lawn chair on one of the piers and began to look around. An inquisitive ring-billed gull appeared from nowhere and flew straight toward me until, within a few yards of my perch, it veered to pick something off the water and then sailed off, its disdain for me apparent.

That gull served as chorus for other life was soon evident. A quarter mile down the shore on another pier stood a half dozen great black-backed gulls and three herring gulls together with other ring-bills. Below them a group of five mergansers paddled quietly in the water.

As the huge orange ball of the sun rose in the east out of the surface mist, other merganser flocks began to appear well out over the lake, mostly as groups of arrow-sharp gray shapes speeding along a few feet above the water surface.

Panning my telescope along the waves, I passed over other gulls bobbing on the surface and stopped when I came upon two loons. I was lucky to find them because they were spending most of their time underwater. I tried to time one dive. At 40 seconds my attention was diverted by a single scaup that flew across my field, but I know that loons often stay down for over a minute and have been recorded remaining underwater for three.

Now other birds appeared. Three Bonaparte's gulls, their flight more buoyant and graceful than their heavier cousins. In contrast a single loon flying awkwardly but powerfully. And then suddenly a group of small white birds bounded into view: 32 snow buntings flying west several hundred yards out over the lake, forerunners of thousands that will follow them along this shore.

My two hours up, I moved my gear back up to the car, returning only for one final look. There almost out of sight going away were about sixty dark shapes. I was tempted to call them brant but they were too far off to be sure.

39. Chasing

As I have pointed out, listing represents the sport of birding. Not highly regarded by many serious ornithologists, it still adds interest, involvement and, yes, competition to this increasingly popular avocation. If you press birders, you can usually get a series of numbers representing totals for their personal lists.

There are even minor rewards. At one time you could send to the Federation of New York State Bird Clubs (now the New York State Ornithological Association) for a jacket patch when your state list has reached 100, another at 200; and the American Birding Association annually publishes the names of those who have achieved regional and international high counts.

Listing is one of the motivations, but not the only one; another is called "chasing," that is, seeking out rare or unusual birds. Non-listers and even non-birders are intrigued when a rare species shows up nearby. A similar interest generates the long lines at zoos when exotic animals like pandas are exhibited.

In support of chasing and more generally to provide information about bird populations, local and state groups offer a variety of services designed to inform birdwatchers when and where to find rare birds. These are provided over the internet and by telephone. For example, here in western New York the Buffalo Ornithological Society today offers several such services. The longest standing is Dial-a-Bird, a weekly-updated phone message for many years supervised by outstanding local birder David Suggs. Earlier Buffalo Museum of Science curator Arthur Clark played this role. You can call 716-896-1271 to hear this report about western New York birds. At this same number local observers are also provided an opportunity to submit their own observations. Similar resources are offered by many other North American communities.

A few years ago a Hotline bird created great excitement. The species enjoys a name as exotic as is the bird itself: ancient murrelet. One spent several days near the Summerville Pier at the mouth of the Genesee River in Rochester.

Murrelets are robin-sized sea birds, members of the alcid family that includes auks, puffins, dovekies and guillemots. The "ancient" of its name is indeed age-related, but the bird itself is not old; rather, its gray back appears like an elderly person's shawl. The ancient murrelet is normally found in the Pacific near our west coast; how it got across the country is anyone's guess.

An occasional chaser myself, I made two unsuccessful trips to Rochester to try to see this bird. Much to the surprise and consternation of local fishermen, each time there were crowds of bird chasers on the pier.

Rochester birder Bob Spahn, who had seen the murrelet, described for me how this miniature penguin look-alike "flew" underwater after schools of minnows. Unintimidated it showed off its fishing skills as dozens of people peered down at it from a few feet away. Through the clear water they watched it dash into a school to grab two small fish. It then surfaced with them still in its bill as if to elicit applause.

Each time I visited, birders had gathered from several states and Canadian provinces. Earlier on one day when they (and I) missed the murrelet by less than an hour, a group of Ontario chasers had first driven to Detroit to see another rarity, a vermillion flycatcher. There they did find that brightly colored bird, which seldom strays far from the Mexican borderlands. But now they were lamenting how, if they had only skipped lunch, they would have arrived in time to see the bird that was eluding us.

You can imagine how I felt: both species would have added to my own life list.

40. Colorado Substitutions

Early in June a few years ago I spent a week at my son's new wilderness vacation home near La Veta, Colorado, ninety miles south of Denver and less than forty miles from the New Mexico border. The house is set in the side of a mountain at 8500 feet, only a few hundred feet from where the pines and spruces among stunted oaks give way to open rock. It was very windy there except in early mornings. It was easy to lose your breath there but the views were spectacular.

Several mornings mule deer passed a few feet from the house and we had to take in the bird feeder at night to avoid attracting bears. I was told that rattlesnakes are common in the nearby rock scree and we found one run over on the road a few hundred yards below the house.

It was early for wildflowers at this altitude, but in nearby meadow openings there were many white racemes of what I believe are death camus. We also found a lovely clump of blue gentians beside the driveway.

It was interesting to compare the bird life there with ours in Western New York. To my surprise, their most common bird is the ubiquitous American robin. Its cheery song was always the first I heard when I ventured out each morning. But this was not the only species we share with the Rockies. Crows constantly flew by, taking advantage of the mountainside updrafts and I also saw and heard a raven, a species regularly seen in our Southern Tier.

The soft calls of local mourning doves were lost in the wind. A male flicker visited an anthill behind the house. Although this is the same species as ours, I could see the red mustache mark that replaces the black of our eastern birds. This bird didn't fly while I was watching or I might have seen its pink wing undersides. That color replaces the yellow that give it the names yellowhammer or yellow-shafted flicker in the East.

Far down the mountain I was surprised to observe a great blue heron wading in a small pond. The only warblers I saw were yellow-rumps.

Those were species we share. More often I found replacement species related to but in most cases quite different from our eastern birds. Here they are:

* Equally fast-flying white-throated swifts substituted for our chimney swifts.

* Our ruby-throated hummingbirds are displaced in the Rockies by broad-tailed hummingbirds. One of these delightful broad-tails buzzed down to light on my hat.

* A dusky flycatcher greeted me one morning with a brief nasal burst. It is one of the Empidonax flycatchers that are so hard to differentiate except by their notes. We have five here in the East: least, willow, alder, Acadian and yellow-bellied. This western species is typical of the chaparral and small trees that surround my son's house.

* Our blue jay is rarely found there. Instead Steller's and pinyon jays fill their niche. They did not yet come to their feeder but they approached to sit atop nearby spruces. (On a visit to Rocky Mountain National Park we found other corvids, Clark's nutcrackers and magpies.)

* Although tree swallows occur in the Rockies, the birds around my son's home were the quite similar violet-green swallows. I had to look closely to see their distinctive white cheeks.

* Among the first songs I heard each morning were the hoarse robin-like phrases of a tanager. Our scarlet tanagers do not occur there; this was a western tanager. I spent an hour finding this beautiful songster, but the time was well spent. Most of the red of the eastern species is replaced by yellow; only its head is red.

* I also recognized another cheery song there. It was like that of our rose-breasted grosbeak, but this was the replacement black-headed grosbeak.

* Several towhees appeared in the bushes around the house. Replacing our Eastern towhee were two species: similar looking spotted towhees and very different appearing green-tailed towhees.

* On a fencepost near one of the alpine meadows sat a Western meadowlark, distinguishable from our eastern species only by its very different song. We rarely see this bird here.

41. Sharpie

A female sharp-shinned hawk has apparently moved into our neighborhood for the winter. My wife and I have seen her several times.

The sharp-shin or sharpie, names by which birders know this species, is a small hawk, males only about the size of a mourning dove, females larger but still not as big as a crow. Appearances can be deceiving, however. Our visitor, her feathers fluffed up against the cold, her fierce intimidating eyes staring back at us when she notices us at a window, looks much larger. To small birds she must look like King Kong.

Indeed, the first time we spotted her, she was on the ground under a neighbor's cedar, peering up into the branches in search of the sparrows that had fled there. It was like an episode from one of those monster movies: the giant creature after tiny prey whose only defense is concealment.

This morning she's in our yard. She has caught one of those sparrows and stands in the snow feeding on it. Although I would not recommend the little hawk's table manners, her breakfast gives us an opportunity to study her at close range.

Our sharpie is an elegant bird. Her back is dark brown except for random feathers that are so white I have to look closely to see they aren't patches of snow. Her under-tail coverts are also snow white and her tail is barred. Her breast is pale with reddish-brown vertical streaks, quite unlike the horizontal rust-colored breast streaking of males. Especially noticeable through binoculars are three bright yellow features: her eyes, the top of her bill and her legs.

The sharp-shinned hawk well deserves its reputation as a "bird hawk." An early 20th century ornithologist examined the stomachs of 159 of these raptors: 52 were empty; all but four of the rest contained birds, among them doves, woodpeckers, swifts, flycatchers, sandpipers, blackbirds, jays, vireos and warblers, thrushes, thrashers and catbirds. This raptor also feeds on mice, shrews, young rabbits, bats, frogs and many insects, but those make up only a small part of its diet. Surprisingly, although they are common where this hawk feeds, kinglets, creepers and chickadees are rarely caught. Perhaps they are too small to interest a hawk: each of them weighs only about as much as two pats of butter.

The sharp-shin's hunting methods are accurately described by the famous early 20th century ornithologist, William Brewster: It "pounces unexpectedly on its victims, after watching for their appearance from an inconspicuous, nearby perch, or seeking them by successive gliding flights of no great length, performed low over the ground. Interrupting such flight merely by an abrupt turn or drop, and then pausing but for an instant, the hawk may continue on its way bearing in its talons some luckless, fear-stupefied warbler or sparrow which has been plucked from twig or turf with truly admirable dexterity. Or it may achieve similar success at the end of a short, spirited dash, made at top speed, and perhaps with reckless disregard of stiff intervening branches." He adds that its passes at prey are "often too quick for the human eye to follow."

Falconers agree with Brewster's characterization of the sharp-shin's reckless disregard: their sharpies often injure themselves plunging after prey into underbrush.

Many sharp-shinned hawks pass through this region while migrating, but in past years few have stayed through the winter. Now, however, the same feeders that help small birds survive this difficult season, provide a ready source of prey for these predators and encourage them to remain here as well.

Watch for sharpies and their larger relatives, Cooper's hawks and goshawks, near feeders. Whether or not you approve of their diet, they are exciting birds to observe.

42. An April Fool Episode

Each year as April First approaches, I consider a pseudoscientific phenomenon that fits the occasion, like those spectacular fakes, Piltdown man and the Cardiff giant. In this essay I address another announced fraud; however, the story ending differs.

First, some background. In 1859 Charles Darwin published his paradigm-changing *Origin of the Species.* In it he expounded the theory of evolution, which according to zoologist Steven Jay Gould is "the basic idea that organisms connect by ties of genealogy."

Just two years later Karl Haberlein discovered a remarkable fossil deposited in a Bavarian limestone mine at the time of the dinosaurs. Two layers of the rock were split apart to display the impression in both surfaces. The fossil was largely reptilian with a long bony tail, but it had feathers, the defining characteristic of birds. Here was an evolutionary connection, a "missing link" between two otherwise distinct classes of life: dinosaurs and birds.

Richard Owen immediately purchased the fossil for the British Museum and assigned it to a new genus, Archaeopteryx. That tongue-twisting spelling challenge is Latin for ancient wing. I consider myself fortunate to be among the many thousands who have visited that museum and seen there those two large flat rocks with their striking impressions of feather and bone.

With this background established we jump ahead a century and a quarter to 1985. Then a group of scientists including the famous British astronomer, Sir Fred Hoyle, announced that Archaeopteryx is a fake. At a scientific meeting and in the scientific literature they claimed that the "fossil" was formed by pressing modern feathers into a layer of artificial cement spread over the genuine imprint of a small dinosaur. Owen, they claimed, participated in the fraud because, as an opponent of evolution, he was "setting a trap" for the Darwinians.

This was not one of those three-headed-aliens stories suitable only for the sensational press of supermarket check-out counters: it made the British *Times* and *Guardian* and was headline news in respected newspapers in this country as well. Creationists — those who reject evolution often for religious reasons — rejoiced: here was a real crack in their opponents' armor.

The debunkers' claim was considered so important that a team of five British Museum scientists headed by anthropologist Alan Charig spent weeks investigating it. Their results, reported in the journal *Science*, reject the fraud charges for many reasons. If glue was spread over one face of the rock, the two faces would not fit perfectly. But they do. There would be a discontinuity between the rock and the cement. There isn't. And fossil parts between the feathers and the rock surface fit matching parts of the other rock face. Finally and most telling, there are now many other Archaeopteryx fossils. Did a team of charlatans continue gluing eleven additional specimens?

The worst aspect of this ridiculous attack was its indictment of Owen, who has for too long been portrayed as a villain of science. A recent fine biography, *Richard Owen: Victorian Naturalist* by Nicolaas Rupke, fully discharges this view. Owen believed that God had both initiated life and established forces to support and extend it. These forces, he believed, included evolution. Thus Owen was in fact an evolutionist who disagreed with Darwinians only about the mechanisms that drove the process. For example, he fully supported the view accepted today that Archaeopteryx is a transitional genus relating birds and dinosaurs. His most vehement Darwinian opponent, T. H. Huxley, did not.

As to the attack itself: "Scientists find themselves in catch-22," says Gould. "If we respond vigorously to an outrageous claim, we stand accused of hysteria. Thus, the most irresponsible ideas often get the best press."

Some might apply this lesson to contemporary politics.

43. Bird Identification Requests

One of the pleasures of my role as a nature columnist was responding to reader inquiries. The most common request took the form: "What kind of bird is this?" followed by a description of one seen in the caller's neighborhood.

Answering is sometimes easy: the caller provides a few general characteristics and responds to a question or two and we have it. A black bird a little larger than a robin with a long v-shaped tail is a common grackle. A small gray-backed bird that creeps downward around tree trunks is one of the nuthatches. A short conversation and a reference to a bird book satisfies both my interrogator and me.

More often the identification is not nearly so simple and provides an interesting challenge. Which reminds me of two stories. Consider them:

William Edson, through the first half of the 20th century the dean of Rochester, New York bird watchers, told me about a caller who insisted she had a Carolina parakeet in her yard. The call came in the early 1940s and the species had been considered extinct since 1914, so Bill was quite reasonably skeptical. But the lady was so certain that she knew her birds and so insistent that he look at this one that Bill, who didn't own a car, rode his bicycle fourteen miles across the city to the woman's home. There he identified the "Carolina parakeet" as a mourning dove.

Richard O'Hara, another fine Rochester birder, was a junior high school teacher in one of that city's schools. One day a student came to him before class in great excitement. "I found a wonderful bird," he said, and he rushed on, "It's red and white and yellow and black and gray and brown and it has a crest."

Dick was naturally perplexed by this description as I was when he told me about this episode. I suggest that experienced birders before reading on pit their own skills against those details.

The student informed his mystified teacher that the bird had died and he promised to bring its body to school the next day. He did so and the bird in hand was immediately identifiable as a cedar waxwing. In his excitement the boy had focused attention on less important details: the waxwing does indeed have a few beads of red on its wings, a yellow fringe at the end of its tail, a white whisker-mark on its face, and so on, but its overall appearance is a tan bird with a black mask and a crest. With that description Dick — and we — would have been home free.

This background brings me to a call I received from a neighbor who had an unusual bird in her yard. Her attention had been drawn to it by her house cats mewing from inside her front screen door. Outside she found a strange looking bird calmly peering in at the interested cats. She described it as about a foot high, walking about on reddish legs. Its back was gray-brown, its sides jailbird-barred black and white. A black line ran through its eye and around a white bib.

The description baffled me so I volunteered to visit and look for it. When I arrived and we immediately found the bird, I saw that the woman's description had been exact. It was a chukar, an Old World quail that hunters tried for years to introduce to this region — never successfully.

Unfortunately this escaped bird would almost certainly not live long. These cats were kept indoors but others in the neighborhood would likely make short work of this ill-prepared escape.

I enjoyed these interactions with readers even when, especially with insects and wildflowers, I must refer them to experts in those fields. Happily they continue to challenge me.

44. South for Hawks

Fifty years ago Rosalie Edge purchased a tract of land that included high rock outcroppings along the Kittatinny Ridge in east-central Pennsylvania. That property — before her purchase a base for shooting hundreds of hawks each fall — became one of the best-known sanctuaries in this country. We now know it as Hawk Mountain.

With Mike Hamilton I visited Hawk Mountain one year in early October. On that weekday afternoon at least fifty people sat on the high rocks or walked along the trails. I had been there before on a weekend when the visitors numbered in the hundreds.

It was a beautiful day, cloudless, pleasantly cool, but the wind was not right for hawks. A northwest or north wind would have swept up mountain contours to bring them sailing by, but that day winds were from the east. Still a few hawks lazily floated over, high in the thermals or low along the ridge.

There were many turkey vultures and we identified two black vultures among them. The black vulture's tail is much shorter, the pattern of white in its wings differs and it flies with less dihedral. Its head is black; the turkey vulture's red, like its namesake the turkey. Even Pennsylvania is beyond the normal range of black vultures: they rarely stray north of the Mason Dixon Line, so these were unexpected sightings.

We also saw an osprey, a red-shouldered hawk, several red-tailed hawks and among the dozen accipiters a sharp-shinned hawk pestering a much larger Cooper's hawk. Just before we left, we had an excellent view of a raven that flapped silently past only a few yards from the lookout.

From Hawk Mountain we drove down to join friends for a week at Cape May, New Jersey, the next-best-known hawk watching spot. A look at the map shows why this peninsula is such a good location for migrant watching in the fall. Although land birds do fly over water, they prefer overland flights and southward migrants along the east coast are funneled between the Atlantic Ocean and Delaware Bay. They accumulate at Cape May before finally venturing out across the open water to Delaware.

At the Cape you don't have to climb a mountain to see hawks. Instead a half dozen steps leads to one of the wooden platforms near the lighthouse at Cape May Point State Park. There with hundreds of others you wait for hawks to pass overhead.

And you don't usually have to wait very long. That fall watchers had already recorded over 22,000 hawks. Among them almost half were sharp-shins, at the time this species making a strong comeback from several years of low numbers.

We had it even easier. Six of us joined Gordon and Diana Bellerby of Niagara-on-the-Lake at the lovely beachfront home they had leased. We had only to sit in lounge chairs on the second floor porch to watch the accipiters and falcons sail by a few feet overhead. On the Niagara Frontier the kestrel is common, the other two falcons rare, but here we were seeing many more peregrine falcons and merlins than kestrels. Occasionally these powerful birds would even rest in nearby trees before beating off along the dunes ever southward.

Hawks were not the only birds on exhibition in Cape May. On a small pond an Eurasian wigeon, a duck I consider more beautiful even than the spectacular wood duck and pintail, drifted quietly, its rosy cheeks and creamy forehead enhanced by the late afternoon sun.

A few warblers and vireos also lingered in copses of live oak, pitch pine and holly, but with all those hawks around they were tough to find.

45. Tidelands

The tidelands of our eastern seashore between Long Island and Georgia are a world apart.

Driving across New Jersey between open pastures quite similar to those of Western New York, we briefly pass through an impenetrable-appearing belt of pine and oak forest and suddenly emerge to find ourselves looking out over miles of salt marsh. These are the tidelands.

Everything is different here.

The sights: A broad vista of cordgrass replaces our marsh cattail. Water channels and mud flats streak browns and blues across the chartreuse meadows. White egrets pose silently or flap lazily overhead.

The sounds: Instead of the strident roar of Niagara River speedboats, we hear the soft sound of distant motors: the unhurried popping of two-cycle engines on flat-bottomed fishing dories or the still deeper chugging of larger tug-shaped craft making their way out to sea. Nighttime brings the hyena cackles of clapper rails.

But most of all the smells: The pungent salt smell borne in by sea breezes is most noticeable, but with it we sense less pleasing odors. Decaying plants and fish, a mix of nitrogen and ammonia compounds, what cooks recognize as that of meat that has "gone off." And sulfur — that same hydrogen sulfide of chem lab — here the foul breath of oxygen-lacking bacteria living in the deep ooze. Partly ameliorating these dismal emanations is the fresh smell of marsh plants, of chlorophyll doing its work. It takes us outsiders some time to get used to this rich brew.

It is difficult to realize that these calm prairies of spartina, these placidly curling channels and creeks and the tranquil oceanfront dunes beyond them represent a harsh and unforgiving region. In some autumns apocalyptic hurricanes bring devastation to the dunes and marshes and destroy beachfront properties, but there are less dramatic yet equally insistent forces at work as well. Constant daytime-onshore, nighttime-offshore winds grind everything with salt and sand. Twice daily tides flood the marshes. Plants and animals here must acclimate to lives half of them soaking in cool brine, half baking in hot sun.

Despite these constraints, the tidelands are rich with life. Salt marshes and estuaries sustain twice as much organic matter per acre as the most fertile agricultural soil. Just one of these acres can support a million fiddler crabs.

At the margin between the dunes and the marshes we watch hundreds of these half-inch crabs scuttle sidewise across the sand. They seem to be everywhere. If all of these tiny arthropods grew to full two-inch size we would be inundated with them. But we needn't worry. The roster of their enemies is endless. Thousands of shorebirds — sandpipers and plovers, turnstones and dunlin, dowitchers and yellowlegs — swarm over the mud flats and beaches, their bills ever probing the mire. Herons and rails stalk the channel edges. Gulls patrol the shore. Other adversaries include larger crustaceans, fish and fishermen.

We watch one gull hunting between beachfront waves. Each time the water retreats it cocks its head and peers about, then dashes to a bubble in the sand to peck out and gobble the still wriggling crab.

There is other plant life here too. In many areas intrusive phragmites has overwhelmed the cordgrass and in sandy spots we find among more familiar goldenrods and pokeweed lovely sea myrtles, sagebrush relatives with cottony white blossoms. Signs of the South are a few sharp-leaved yuccas and prickly pear cacti. And at inshore marsh edges bayberries abound. Every chance I get I break off a twig to smell its lovely after-shave fragrance.

Each time I visit the tidelands I find myself more spellbound by this remarkable ecological region, so unlike our own.

46. Bird Feeder Problems

Will this be a good year for feeding birds? I will stock up on sunflower seeds, suet and millet and prepare for the best!

Or will it be bad year? Having suffered myself, I derive some pleasure from the many stories I hear of bird feeding problems.

My favorite is the "too much of a good thing" problem. Bird watchers are delighted when the first evening grosbeaks show up. Their noisy belligerence is entertaining. But their hosts soon learn that they are voracious eaters. Birdseed orders rise from quarts to bushels. The welcome soon wears thin and folks begin to shoo grosbeaks away to save food for less bellicose cardinals and dickeybirds.

Another problem is what has been described to me as the "Walmart effect." After several seasons of enjoying a wide variety of birds at your feeders suddenly none appear. Attracted by a display at a store, your neighbor has joined the feeding community and attracted your birds with dozens of trays and tubes and suet bags. Sadly you attribute faithlessness to those you thought were your feathered friends.

But worst of all, hands down, is the problem of squirrels. What bird feeder has not met this problem head on — only to be humbled by the pesky rodents? They not only drive away the birds and eat all their food, but they also gnaw through and destroy your expensive equipment.

"Squirrel proof the tree in which you mount your feeder," the advertisement read. I bought the metal ring and wrapped it around the black birch that held ours only to watch our local denizen, Mr. S, nonchalantly step over the useless device as though it wasn't there.

That made me so angry I climbed high up into the tree and hung the feeder from a 30-foot wire. To no avail, the next morning Mr. S was again coiled inside, his protruding tail twitching as he gobbled sunflower seeds. Later I watched him climb to a limb at least fifteen feet above the feeder from which he jumped down onto the feeder roof.

"I'll fix that bugger," I thought. I took down the feeder and drove long nails out through the roof boards. It looked like a pin cushion. "Jump on this," I snarled as I rehung it.

But then, of course, I had misgivings. Surely this represented a procrustean response. That night I dreamt of Iron Marys and other medieval torture chambers.

Early the next morning I rushed out to remove the nails. Too late! Mr. S was back, uninjured and again reclining in the feeder stuffing himself. I swear he grinned at me.

I admitted defeat that day and have resentfully tolerated Mr. S and his relatives ever since.

47. Christmas Meeting

Pari was born last June. For twelve days before that her tiny body had developed inside a five-eighths inch pinkish egg freckled with brown. On her birthday she pecked at her confining wall until finally she emerged into a dimly lighted world.

The chickadee's Reinstein Woods Sanctuary home in Cheektowaga, New York was a hollow in a dying white birch. Using their beaks like woodpeckers, her parents had drilled a hole through the tree's bark and cambium into rotten heartwood. There her mother hollowed out an inner chamber, eating the carpenter ant larva she found in the pulp as she worked. Finally satisfied with the nest size, she lined its floor with moss, molted feathers and deer hair.

Pari was the last to emerge from her shell. She found herself crowded among six siblings, their bodies warmed by her mother's tummy with its surrounding breast feather quilt. Soon her instincts drove the tiny chick to join her brothers and sisters, mouths agape, begging for food.

Fortunately food was plentiful. The harried parents spent the next two weeks dashing about, gathering arthropod eggs and larva, many of them tent caterpillars, from nearby trees and carrying them to their ever-demanding offspring. Occasionally this diet was complemented with poison ivy berries that had lasted through the winter and hearts of sunflower seeds stolen from an odd glass-lined box that somehow produced an unlimited supply.

Last to hatch, Pari was also last to leave the nest. When she did she looked like a slightly shaggier version of her parents: her back slate gray; her breast and cheeks white; her throat, crown and eyes vivid black. That crown gives her species its name: black-capped chickadee.

Then began Pari's lifetime of acrobatics. She soon learned from her parents how to find food by examining leaves, needles and the rough bark of tree limbs for insects and their eggs, and watching the grass below for spiders active in their webs and skippers feeding on wildflowers. She needed that food-finding skill to fuel her spirited flights, her spontaneous midair twists and turns, her impossible landings upside-down on the tiniest of twigs, all accompanied by her almost continuous cheery *dee-dee-dee* calls.

Patty is a child of another species. She could scarcely be more unlike Pari. A human child born to a life of beds and wheelchairs, Patty is fortunate to have deeply devoted parents. Her life defines restriction just as Pari's does freedom, yet Patty is a happy three-year old. Her parents provide loving care and she enjoys vicariously the activities of her older brother, Paul.

Today Patty and Pari will meet.

This morning Patty's family ventures out into the snow to try out the children's presents. They drive to Stiglmeier Park in Cheektowaga where Paul dons his cross-country skis and Patty is carefully tucked onto her sled. Off they go into the woods where cardinals whistle, juncos feed along the footpath and tame deer wander just yards away.

The time Patty has been waiting for arrives. Her father carefully removes one of her mittens, turns over her hand to form a cup and places in it a single sunflower seed. He steps back. Now it is her family's turn to watch Patty.

An itinerant flock of chickadees and kinglets approaches. Among them is Pari, who sees the child in her bright red snowsuit, her hand offering the luscious morsel.

Down Pari drops to a low branch and without hesitation flits to the child's hand to take the seed. Her tiny claws make momentary tingling contact with Patty's palm and the little girl giggles with delight.

For Patty and her family — and, may we hope, for Pari too — that instant marks the high point of a Christmas morning to remember.

48. Fred Hall

In 2015 Buffalo Audubon celebrated the 40th anniversary of the Fred T. Hall Nature Center at Beaver Meadow. In partial repayment for his kindness to me personally I offer here a brief summary of Fred's life.

Born and raised in Crawfordsville, Indiana, Hall developed an early interest in wildlife. By his teens he had accumulated one of the finest butterfly collections in the state. Despite his parents' lack of funds to send him to college, he was encouraged by a family friend to try the entrance examination for the nearby Wabash College. Hall was not only accepted but won a scholarship and was able to enroll. Soon he was hired as a lab assistant in the college biology department and passed his scholarship on to another deserving student.

After graduation Hall joined the staff of Ward's Natural Science Establishment in Rochester. And it was there that I met him. As a junior high school student, I joined his ornithology class at the Rochester Science Museum. It was a wonderful experience. I was by about twenty years the youngest member of the course and Hall paid special attention to me. He even allowed me to take home the remarkable sketches he made of various bird characteristics. Only later did I learn that he was a highly regarded artist. Unfortunately over time those sketches were lost.

Then came World War II. Hall went through officer training and was commissioned an army captain. He received what was arguably the best assignment of that war: recreation officer in Bermuda.

While he was there, Hall continued his natural history interests and even gained an international reputation in ornithology. He found on a beach the recent skeleton of a sea bird believed to be extinct at the time, a cahow or Bermuda petrel. Although he was transferred shortly after this important discovery, his identification led others to find a few of these extremely rare birds that come ashore for only brief visits to underground caves on rocky outcrops. (See essay 22.)

After the war Hall returned to Ward's but he was soon appointed director of the Davenport, Iowa Public Museum. In 1950 he finally came here to serve for 19 years until his early death as director of the Buffalo Museum of Science.

Hall was probably best known here for his weekly live show, "Your Museum of Science," which ran for years. He took many 16 mm movies that he used to illustrate those programs and his family donated some of those films to the museum. And here is where our paths crossed again. In the 1990s as a museum volunteer I went through those films. Although they included many family episodes, they also recorded rare birds, plants and animals he found here, thus contributing scientific evidence.

When Fred Hall died, James Mason, president of the museum honored him: "He was learned in a wide variety of science disciplines, he wrote and lectured on ornithology, botany, entomology and nature photography. His distinguished characteristic was, however, the warmth of his personality, and it was this trait that made him a truly great teacher. Despite his full schedule and the arduous duties of director, he always found time to devote to the groups of school children visiting the museum. He displayed a native empathy with young people and instilled in them an awareness of the natural world as well as his own deeply held conviction of the importance of conservation."

Jim Hall, Fred's son and a Hamburg horticulturist, confirmed this, telling me how his dad took his wife and five children to visit 45 of our 50 states. "He was," Jim added, "the brightest man I have ever known."

49. Shrike

I first catch sight of the bird as it flies low over the Iroquois National Wildlife Refuge marsh. It is robin-sized, gray, and it flashes white patches in its dark wings as it beats purposefully over the reeds and a broad snow covered pond. My first thought is mockingbird. But when it reaches the line of tall trees and swoops effortlessly up, up, up to perch on the tip of the highest branch, I know that this is my first Northern shrike of the winter.

Excited to find this uncommon visitor from the spruce forests of northern Labrador, I focus my binoculars on it. It has black wings and tail, a soft gray back and crown, and a finely barred white breast. But most noticeable are its black mask and the hooked raptorial bill that identifies this songbird as a predator.

As I watch, the shrike bends its head to look in my direction. Sighting something, it sails steeply down to a dogwood bush only twenty feet from me. Oblivious to my presence it stares at the ground where the fickle wind has cleared snow from a small area.

Suddenly the shrike drops to the ground and I can see it grasp something brown at the edge of the snowdrift. It beats its wings several times to provide the leverage to drag a big meadow vole out into the open.

But the exposed field mouse quickly breaks out of the clutches of the shrike and turns on its assailant. This is not an unequal battle as the mouse is bigger than the torso of the shrike and clearly outweighs its opponent. Fierce and aggressive, it springs at the shrike several times. The bird retreats before each of these onslaughts, but it fends off the mouse's thrusts with sharp blows from its hawk-like bill.

For a time the outcome appears uncertain, but then the mouse seems to tire and it stops its attacks. The combatants face each other for a long moment, but the shrike stares down its opponent and the mouse turns to dash for safety under the snow.

It doesn't make it! In a flash the shrike springs to the mouse's back and digs its bill deep into the rodent's neck. All is over quickly. The mouse twitches twice and then is still.

The shrike now grasps the big mouse with its bill and feet and takes off toward the woods. I continue to watch it until it disappears behind the trees. All that are left behind are a few drops of blood rapidly congealing on the snow.

Only now do I realize that I have been standing perfectly still through this entire drama. A chill sweeps up my back and the aching of my cold fingers becomes apparent. I must move on to prevent hypothermia in the biting cold. I trudge ahead, my snowshoes sinking into the very light snow with that squeak, squeak, squeak familiar to winter hikers.

But the episode is not quite complete. The trail along the levee leads to a patch of woods. There a single honeylocust still retains a few of its long seedpods. However, that is not what captures my attention. Impaled on one of the tree's big thorns is the body of the vole. On another is a junco, similarly impaled. The shrike has cached its victims here for later feeding and has flown off in search of other prey. This behavior — hanging its victims like carcasses in a butcher's shop — gives the shrike another name: butcherbird.

Now to my surprise a tiny chickadee flies up and begins to peck at the vole's stiffening carcass. Obviously any food source is to be utilized in the frigid temperatures of this winter.

50. Alternate Treats

When I was an eleven year-old beginning birder, I found late February and early March the worst time of year. All winter I had studied bird books, learning about bird habits and memorizing their characteristics for identification. I had started a year list with the few winter birds I found in our neighborhood. Bird feeders were not yet in vogue so that list only included species like house sparrow, crow, chickadee and downy and hairy woodpecker. It did include, as I recall, one less common species: pine siskin. There had been an incursion that winter.

I could not wait for the migration to commence so that I could add to my list. I had a goal of reaching a hundred species for the year and I was a bundle of nerves in anticipation. I wandered the fields and wooded areas behind my home and trekked to nearby parks. Not a single new bird. It wasn't until weeks later that robins and song sparrows and red-winged blackbirds and grackles arrived and a snipe whose wings produced its *who-who-who* sound over the open field behind our neighborhood.

Last week my thoughts returned to those frantic days as I walked the trails of Golden Hills State Park east of Olcott on Lake Ontario. Except for the sound of the wind the woods and fields were silent. Only a few crows and gulls flew overhead. It was a bright sunny day, a perfect morning for a walk, but I felt unusually isolated.

Then, however, that didn't bother me. There was much to be seen. Now as an adult I was no longer so tightly focused on birds that I paid little attention to other aspects of the world around me. With few birds in evidence I could still enjoy the hike.

Succession was occurring on this recently farmed land. Most stages were apparent: overgrown fields, brush lots, groups of young trees fighting for dominance, but few fully mature trees. Along the trail I followed, park employees had placed signs to describe these ecological stages. I found these posters informative and well prepared. I learned from one, for example, that foresters call early succession woodlots pole stands.

With few birds and animals to observe, I could turn my attention to other things. I tested the brown flower heads of Queen Anne's lace to see if all the seeds were gone. Only a few remained. The rest were off seeking soil for germination. On a goldenrod stem were two of those spherical tumors that are the plant's response to the larva of goldenrod gall flies. One had a hole in its side where a bird, most likely a chickadee, had drilled through to feed on the insect. The other was undisturbed. I opened it with my penknife and there was the little fly larva. Why didn't the chickadee drill out that one too?

Now after a few warm days most of the snow was gone. The trail passed without warning from frozen dirt to squishy muck and the standing water was covered with only a thin slick of ice. From a few yards down the trail it looked black, but as I approached it seemed to disappear and I could see the grass and mud underwater. Only where trapped air made amoeba-like white areas was the surface evident. When I stepped on it, however, the ice announced itself. Crackling sounds raced off across the surface like streaks of heat lightening.

I pushed my way off the trail into a pine grove to look for saw-whet owls. No luck, but I did find on a leafless tamarack a thick growth of twigs called a witch's broom. It is the tree's reaction to some kind of viral, fungus or mite infection.

Just as in those days of my youth I didn't add to my year list of bird species but now, more relaxed, I found much else on which to focus my thoughts. The birds would arrive soon enough.

51. Early Spring Hawks

My wife and I took advantage of one of those rare spring days at the end of March to drive down along the Lake Ontario shore.

Doris is a great partner on these drives as she plays the role of bird spotter. Even though she drives, she is always the first to see birds. Each time a predictable dialogue follows.

"There's a hawk."

"Where?"

"There, just over those trees and below those small clouds."

"Which trees? Which clouds? There are hundreds of each."

As a further aid, Doris now points, her index finger blunted against the car window indicating approximately half the sky.

Sometimes I never do locate the bird and I am told that it went over the horizon or down into the field or behind the trees, but usually I finally see a tiny dot. In my binoculars the speck resolves into a hawk or vulture — or just as often a crow or jay.

On that drive we did not see many hawks. Although the afternoon was clear, the sun bright and the temperature mild, the light breeze was out of the northeast, not conducive to migrating raptors. Mostly we saw only resident red-tailed hawks and kestrels.

That is not a complaint. I always enjoy watching these extreme representatives of our local birds of prey. The red-tail is a big powerful buteo, a slow flier with broad wings and a fanned tail. The kestrel is a tiny falcon smaller than a blue jay, its sharp wings giving it great agility and speed.

On this day we would observe only one other hawk species.

As we approached the lake, we noticed what appeared to be white smoke rolling along the Ontario shoreline. Could all that come from the Somerset Power Plant? Indeed it could not.

The tall stack was emitting only a tiny wisp of smoke. What we were seeing was fog rising from the lake. And at Shadigee we suddenly passed from bright sunlight into that eerie cloud with visibility less than 50 yards.

Retreating back to Route 18, we found Canada Geese feeding noisily in cornfields. From another field rose a big raptor, even larger than a red-tail. It was a rough-legged hawk.

This species is seen here regularly but not commonly in winter and during migration. In late May this bird will nest probably on a shale cliff in the northernmost reaches of Canada.

I ticked off field marks as it hovered just yards away. White rump. Broad black tail band. Dark wing knuckles. White windows in primaries. When it dropped down into the field I could even see the feathered 'long pants' that give it its name. Other hawks' legs are bare.

Returning home through the Clarence turf farms, we came upon two more rough-legs and these birds put on a spectacular show for us.

We first saw them sitting in the lone poplar out in the broad grasslands. Both were dark-phase birds. Melanism is rather common in hawks and these appeared almost as black as crows.

A joker in a pick-up truck drove past honking, mischievously trying to scare them off. He succeeded only in part, the hawks rising majestically to sail in narrow circles over the field.

They were obviously courting, their soaring loops almost intersecting. When they approached each other they would heel over on their sides and flash their talons toward their partner. I hoped that we would see them grasp 'hands' like we saw the Iroquois eagles do several years ago, but they never got quite close enough.

Their acrobatics provided a perfect final act for another pleasant outing on the Niagara Frontier.

On our way home I told Doris about one of my earliest experiences with hawks. Dick O'Hara, Bob Dolan and I were birding along Lake Ontario just west of Rochester. I was driving and let them out at one end of a half mile beach. Our plan was simple: they would walk the beach while I drove around to pick them up at the other end.

But my drive back from the lake turned exciting. I came upon a huge all-white hawk sitting calmly on a fence post at roadside. Gyrfalcon, I thought, and I raced to pick up my friends to add their confirmation to my observation. By the time we returned, however, the hawk was gone from its post and my heart sank. But then it rose up out of the field where it had caught a mouse. In flight the white was broken by dark areas in the wing bends that characterized it not as a gyr but as a light phase rough-legged hawk. It would be years before I saw my first gyrfalcon but that beautiful rough-leg remains to this day one of my favorite sightings.

52. Attracting Hummingbirds

Ruby-throated hummingbirds, those tiny green jewels of rural, suburban and occasionally even urban gardens of the eastern United States, generally return to my New York area on about May first. If you wish to attract them to your yard, prepare for their arrival a few weeks in advance of their arrival date for your area.

These tiny birds will have completed a migration that began weeks ago when they set out from Costa Rica to fly north across the Gulf of Mexico. An ornithologist once argued that they had to ride across the gulf on the backs of large birds like eagles because they were too small to make such a long flight on their own, but it is clear now that their remarkable accomplishment is unaided by that interesting trick.

Although the rest of their trip is less strenuous, they will arrive here with fat supplies seriously depleted. They desperately need such food as nectar and small insects. In some years with the seasons set back by a protracted winter, they will be hard pressed to find these necessary resources. On years like this I have even seen hummingbirds feeding at sapsucker drill holes.

To help these tiny birds and to lure them to your yard, hang out baskets of bright red fuchsias or impatiens and hummingbird nectar feeders. You can find these enticing food sources in garden stores or you can make feeders by painting chemistry test tubes red and mounting them with wire. (Bring flower baskets inside if frost is predicted.)

To make nectar simply add a quarter cup of cane sugar to a cup of boiling water. Don't use honey as it is the wrong kind of sugar.

These suggestions and many of those that follow are taken from an information packed book, *Hummingbird Gardens* by Nancy L. Newfield and Barbara Nielson. It is rich with anecdotes gathered from those who feed hummingbirds across the country.

I hope that many readers will wish to go beyond the emergency measures I have indicated. You can easily modify your gardens to make them attractive to hummingbirds and many of the flowers you set out will serve butterflies as well.

First some general recommendations:

(1) Although hummingbirds will feed on blue and even white flowers, they are most attracted to bright red. Be sure to include red, pink or orange flowers in your garden. Color alone is not enough, however, as flowers like red roses do not provide ample nectar.

(2) In addition to engaging flowers, large trees and shrubs are necessary for hummingbird shelter and nesting habitat.

(3) Choose flowers with staggered blooming times. Although spring bloomers will serve now, you will need summer and fall blossoms to retain and maintain your visitors. Even if you fail to get hummers early in the year, fall flowers may draw southbound migrants and young birds to your garden. Also watch in fall for that rare visitor from the west, the rufous hummingbird.

(4) Keep your yard pesticide free or you will injure these tiny birds. They will return the favor by providing insect and especially mosquito control. If you still face specific insect problems, use mild but effective insecticidal soap.

(5) During dry periods provide shallow water for bathing.

Finally some planting suggestions: Flowering quince, lilac and autumn olive serve early nectar. Summer flowers include bee balm, red-hot-poker, foxglove, hollyhock, Mexican sunflower, daylily, salvia and jewelweed. Add shrubs like butterfly bush; vines like trumpet creeper, red morning glory and honeysuckle; and trees like crabapple and horse chestnut. Among late bloomers are viburnum, phlox and cardinal flower.

Color your garden with handsome flowers and you should attract these feisty iridescent flying jewels.

53. Refuge Census

Iroquois National Wildlife Refuge is best known as a migratory stopover and breeding area for waterfowl. It and sibling refuges across this country and Canada were established to support duck and game hunting. Appropriately much of the funding for their purchase and maintenance derives from federal hunting licenses.

That Iroquois fulfills this purpose is evident not only to hunters in autumn but also to the ever-increasing numbers of western New Yorkers who visit the refuge near Easter time to observe the spring migration. Each year they witness tens of thousands of Canada Geese, hundreds of ring-necked ducks, mallards, teal, wigeon, pintails, wood ducks, shovelers and gadwalls, and dozens of tundra swans. What observer will forget the long skeins of geese overhead, loudly honking flocks on the water and individuals performing wing-up air releases — stunts mimicked by human skydivers — as they drop down to the ponds?

But these areas serve many other purposes as well. The reputation of Iroquois, for example, has been further enhanced by its black tern census, its osprey hacking, its loosestrife control project and its resident eagles observed on visitor center television.

Now, with passerine (that is perching or song bird) populations threatened, the important role of these federal refuges in providing nesting habitat is also being recognized. A national passerine monitoring program has been initiated, each refuge to carry out an annual count following strict rules to insure statistically valid data. The project goals are not only to inventory these passerines, but also to record their relative abundance and changes over the years, to note their distribution among habitats and to identify needed management responses.

Iroquois personnel established sixty census points and carried out their first census early in the new century. This past week Blake Reeves and I completed the second.

We hit three perfect mornings: cool, untypically rain free and with little or no wind. Reversing normal working hours, our days in the field were five to nine — a.m. It was a perfect time for bird watching: the woods and marshes resounded with birdcalls.

Blake identified and I recorded, our tasks keeping us so busy that I came away with little sense of overall populations. Only when we tabulated totals did the evidence come together.

The two most common of the 54 recorded species were yellow warblers and red-winged blackbirds. Together they made up a fifth of the birds tabulated. Next came song sparrows and grackles, followed in declining order of number recorded by yellowthroat, catbird, Baltimore oriole, swamp sparrow, redstart, wood thrush, tree swallow, robin, crested flycatcher, veery and cardinal.

The species that most surprised me was the Baltimore oriole. (Happily its name had recently been returned from northern oriole to this older and more familiar designation.) I had never found this species as widespread as that year; at Iroquois we heard their cheery whistles at almost half the stations.

Of equal interest were some rarer species. We found yellow-billed and black-billed cuckoos, yellow-bellied and Acadian flycatchers. I am concerned by the scarcity of field birds despite many stops near meadows. We recorded only a few field sparrows, one meadowlark and not a single savannah, grasshopper or Henslow's sparrow.

Passerines were, of course, not all we found. Bitterns pumped and grebes cowed in the marshes. A moorhen family, even the young, already with red face plates, skittered off through the reeds. Fields were strewn with buttercups, Indian paintbrush and anemones. Deer posed in the morning mist.

And two giant snapping turtles were finishing a night of egg laying on one of the dikes. Only yards away raccoons had dug up and eaten another batch of turtle eggs.

Sadly, shortly after that pleasant adventure, Blake Reeves began his decline that would take his life, but I would continue those counts with Gail Seamans for several more years.

54. Hawk Encounters

In just one week I enjoyed three unusual experiences with hawks.

The first took place in City Hall. While waiting for a meeting of the Buffalo Pest Management Board to convene, I asked Bill Nowak of the Council staff if he knew where the nest of the peregrine falcons was located.

"Just listen," he responded.

Sure enough, when I tuned out the conversations around me, I could hear the harsh screeching of young birds. They were calling from somewhere just below our fourteenth floor meeting room. Only the unmanageable windows prevented us from seeing the nest.

After the meeting I walked out into Niagara Square and looked up at the towering building. I still couldn't see the aerie but, as I watched, one of the adult peregrines sailed out across the Square and over the Statler Building.

Peregrine means wandering and it is wonderful to have these handsome, swift-flying wanderers back from near extinction. They, like eagles and ospreys, were severely impacted by DDT, which, before it was outlawed, persisted in the bodies of its victims and accumulated in predators like these that feed on birds and mammals lower in the food chain. The falcon's eggshells were so weakened that no young were produced for years.

Now, with human help, these canyon dwellers are returning not only to cliffs like those of the Hudson River Palisades but also to man-made canyons like ours in downtown Buffalo. Here they'll serve as a minor control on the city's population of pigeons, gulls and starlings.

Two days later I learned of another falcon, a kestrel, that has adopted a Tonawanda family. That evening Mike Galas and I visited Bill and Ida Barrett, who lived near Cardinal O'Hara High School in Tonawanda. We had hardly taken seats on their back porch when the robin-sized hawk they call

Freddie the Freeloader sailed up into their ash tree. Mrs. Barrett brought out a small piece of sirloin and tossed it high in the air. The brightly colored red and gray hawk immediately flew out after the meat, but he embarrassed himself on this first pass. It slipped from his grasp. Minutes later, however, he successfully handled the next toss and beat his way purposefully off to a distant perch. There he began to tear at it with his hooked bill.

Freddie had been coming to the Barretts' home for several years, but this was the first he had remained for the summer. No wonder he joined this family. Who among us can claim regular servings of steak tartare?

The very next night as Doris and I were eating supper at our favorite Italian restaurant on Evans Street in Amherst, one of the owners stopped at our table to say that he had something to show us.

Ever game, we followed him out through the kitchen to the back of the building. From the doorway we looked up at an adult red-tailed hawk perched just twenty feet away on a utility pole. The big buteo returned our stares, clearly not intimidated by our presence.

Our host dodged back inside for a moment and reappeared with a raw chicken-wing. As soon as he held it up, the red-tail swooped down, grasped it, and flew back to his perch, where he proceeded to devour meat and bones in about three gulps. Satisfied for the moment, he sailed off to a distant tree.

I find it quite remarkable how these three hawks have adapted to their unusual human contacts. And I am delighted to see how, in these cases at least, people have responded so affectionately to these wildest of birds.

55. Birds Attacking Predators

Anyone who spends time outdoors has probably seen examples of what can only be termed reckless behavior. A soaring or perched hawk harassed by a kingbird or robin. Chickadees, nuthatches, titmice and kinglets mobbing a screech-owl. A clamorous flock of crows chasing a great horned owl. Common terns dive bombing a great black-backed gull approaching their colony.

That kingbird or those terns will even attack us if we approach their nests.

Bird watchers take advantage of small birds' interest in picking on an owl in daytime. They whistle or play a recording of a screech-owl's whinnying call to attract these so-called dickeybirds. Often a dozen or two of the little birds approach to join the action.

Most owls are at a particular disadvantage in daytime. (The daytime-hunting hawk owl and snowy owl are exceptions.) The eyes of our more common owls are designed for night vision and daytime finds them blinking or with their eyes shut. Having completed their night shift, they seek only to sleep through the day.

Other big birds, especially when flying, are at a different kind of disadvantage. They are like ponderous World War II bombers attacked by Japanese Zeros, German Messerschmitts, British Spitfires or our own Wildcats and Thunderbolts.

Like those fighter planes the smaller bird has greater aerodynamic control and speed and it can attack from above or behind. It may even light on the larger bird's back to deliver painful pecks. The hawk's common defense is usually to leave the area. It responds to those pecks by briefly folding its wings and dropping a few feet.

Why do birds do this? Not enjoying special insight into avian minds, I can only conjecture by comparison with our own responses. First is defense of their nest. Of course a better response might well be to keep quiet and let natural camouflage do its work, but we should at least give the birds credit for their concern.

More likely, I think that the source of this behavior is simply testosterone-driven showing off. Look at me, the daredevil. I can take on these ogres many times my size.

The larger birds are not, however, entirely defenseless. Former *USA Today* science columnist, April Holladay, once answered this reader inquiry: "How come big birds don't take a whack at little birds harassing them?" Her answer was that they do occasionally turn on their tormentors and the result is often very serious.

Maurice Braun, former director of Hawk Mountain in Pennsylvania, told this story: "Lying on my back and scanning the zenith, I picked up a small hawk making frequent passes at a much larger, dark bird, annoying its fellow traveler. The dark bird proved to be an adult golden eagle. It made a sudden thrust forward, executed an Immelmann turn [that's a fighter pilot maneuver] as effortlessly as a fly landing on a ceiling, and then, to my amazement, it seized the smaller hawk, which seemed to put up a momentary, hopeless struggle. Down came the two birds precipitously, the eagle with set wings and clutching its victim. As the eagle plunged to earth, the wings of the smaller bird were fully outstretched, and I glimpsed the ruddy breast of the red-shouldered hawk. The eagle, still clutching its prey, disappeared into the densely wooded flank of the ridge."

Bruce Ostrow told of another event: "I noticed a red-tailed hawk and an American crow fly out of the trees. The crow was chasing the hawk and repeatedly attacking the hawk's tail from above. When the hawk and crow approached it, an eagle flew directly at the pair. The hawk dived out of the way, but the crow did not have time to evade the eagle. The eagle grabbed the crow head-on with its talons, killing it instantly."

These episodes were rare enough to warrant reports in ornithological journals. Yet European ornithologist Eberhard Curio reported 35 cases of predators turning on harassers.

Why are these predator responses to these attacks so few in number? Holladay's answer: the predator normally does not strike mobbers because maneuvering in mid-air costs energy, and does not benefit it sufficiently.

We usually think of the big bird as the playground bully and to root for its smaller attacker, but nature does not show our kind of favoritism.

56. Rare Hummingbird

It was an interesting coincidence.

I had received a form letter from the editor of the forthcoming *Birds of New York State*, asking those of us who had provided species accounts to make a final check for recent reports as the deadline for submission of the text to a printer was fast approaching. And the very next day I received a phone call with the news that a rufous hummingbird had appeared at Jim Wojewodzki's feeder in Colden. It was the rarest of the species for which I was responsible.

In the first three editions of Peterson's *Birds of the Eastern United States* the ruby-throated hummingbird was the only hummingbird species included. You had to travel to Texas and farther west to see the other dozen and a half species. But then a few unusual hummers began to appear at eastern feeders in late summer and fall. All ruby-throated hummingbirds are emerald green and white, with the males displaying a brilliant red throat. On these new birds much of that green is replaced by reddish-brown.

Wojewodzki's hummingbird was the 13th of these western birds that had been reported in New York State, all since 1980. Unfortunately only two of the earlier reports were accepted by the state Avian Records Committee. The approved records came from Orange and Washington counties in eastern New York, the first just three years earlier.

The reason the other reports were not accepted is that the rufous hummingbird and another species, Allen's hummingbird, are extremely difficult to differentiate. In many plumages they look very similar. As I write this, for example, I have the National Geographic Society field guide open to the plate showing these two species. Even in the enlarged portrayal I cannot distinguish the difference between the tail patterns of females and the accompanying description says that adult females are inseparable in the field. Thus, although the Allen's hummingbird is a more sedentary species whose normal range is restricted to coastal California, the identification of these birds has usually been accepted only to genus and they have been recorded as "Selasphorus species." In 1990 a number of us drove to Grimsby, Ontario to catch a brief glimpse of one of those indistinguishable Selasphorus hummingbirds.

A few days after the initial report of the Colden visitor, Nora Lindell and I drove down to Wojewodzki's home to see if his hummingbird was still around. Jim's long driveway was lined with cars and we joined a crowd of birders on his back porch. We hardly had time to greet friends when a tiny bird flew to a twig in a nearby treetop. We all focused binoculars on the exquisite little male, its orange-red gorget flashing in the bright sunlight, its rufous back clearly distinguishing it from a ruby-throat.

The little hummingbird dropped down to a syrup feeder and Dick Byron ticked off field marks he saw through his telescope: "A few green feathers among the brown in its back, white spot behind the eye, black feather tips on the tail,..." We all agreed that this was an unmistakable rufous hummingbird, a spanking new addition to the fauna of western New York, but we would still have to wait to see what the records committee would decide. That process takes months since written reports must be accumulated and committee members from across the state polled.

It has been suggested that this hummer be mist-netted for positive identification and the captured bird then transported south for release near the Mexican border. Sadly, if that is not done, its chance of survival through a western New York winter is virtually nil.

Happily I can write now that the record was accepted and the rufous hummingbird was added to the avifauna of western New York.

57. Imperial Woodpecker

One of the thrills of backyard bird feeding is the appearance at your suet feeder of a crow-sized woodpecker with a flaming red crest: a real-life version of the cartoon Woody Woodpecker.

This visitor is a pileated woodpecker, that surname pronounced like pile or pill depending on your personal preference. (I find myself alternating.) You more often see their work on woodland hikes: inches-wide cavities torn out of tree boles or even tree stumps literally torn apart, in both cases the result of their search for the beetles that are doing the real violence to the trees' periderm.

Away from feeders you seldom see these shy birds and when you do it is usually in the distance flying off, but you can identify them from the similar appearing all-black crows by their white underwings. More often you hear their flicker-like but louder and more irregular calls, which the current Peterson guide describes as *kik-kik-kikkik-kik-kik*, etc.

A relative of the pileated woodpecker, a similar appearing but larger species, made headlines after a brief film of a bird identified as an ivory-billed woodpecker was taken by Gene Sparling on April 25, 2004 in the Cache River National Wildlife Refuge of eastern Arkansas. Then a few visitors to the area claimed to have seen additional individuals.

This was indeed big news for the species had been declared extirpated from the North American mainland, the last previous observation having been in 1944. Not to be outdone, a five-member team of ornithologists from Auburn University and the University of Windsor observed what they thought was an ivory-billed woodpecker in a mature swamp forest along the Choctawhatchee River in Florida on May 21, 2005.

Many birders remain unconvinced that these records are acceptable. If nothing else, however, the episodes have led to heightened federal conservation efforts in the regions where those observations took place.

And now we have another related episode. The ivory-bill is (or was) a large version of the pileated woodpecker, but today we have a still larger species in the news. The likely extirpated imperial woodpecker of Mexico, described by Tim Gallagher of the Cornell Laboratory of Ornithology as "the mightiest woodpecker that ever lived," was never known to have been photographed. All the evidence that remained of the species was museum bird skins.

To gain some sense of the size of this mighty bird, consider some measurements: the pileated woodpecker is about 17 inches long, the imperial 23 inches long. That means that the imperial woodpecker would weigh over twice as much as the pileated. It is indeed a big bird since the pileated woodpecker is already crow-sized.

Martjan Lammertink came across some correspondence that identified a Pennsylvania dentist, William Rhein, who had photographed a female imperial woodpecker in 1956. Lammertink and Gallagher contacted Rhein and obtained the film. Although it is of poor quality, it clearly identifies the bird. You can watch the two-minute episode at www.youtube.com/watch?v=Q0OCd6b1aXU.

Excited by their finding, Lammertink and Gallagher traveled to the Sierra Madre in Durango, where Rhein's film was taken, to look for the species. Unfortunately, the area near the village of Guacamayita, is largely controlled by the Los Zetas drug cartel and at the time of their expedition conditions had deteriorated with a wave of violence and crime including kidnappings. Despite this the team spent two weeks looking for the birds, unfortunately with no luck. They even found that local foresters had been poisoning them, believing that they were destroying valuable lumber.

Absent these other remarkable birds, we should remain happy with our pileated woodpeckers.

58. Shorebirds

Many birds are spectacular travelers and none are better defined by their peregrinations than the sandpipers, plovers and related species generally categorized as shorebirds. Almost forty of them are to be observed here each year and the best time to see them is right now. We are already well into their southward fall migration period which extends from July to October.

Consider just one typical species, the pectoral sandpiper, a familiar bird on regional mud flats each fall. Smaller than a robin, this bird enjoyed the winter well down in South America, then spent April and early May flying north to the most remote fringes of northwestern North America. No sooner did it compete its nesting responsibilities than it headed back south again. This southward trip is often described as more leisurely, because the species is to be found here through late summer and fall, but it is still a trip of about 9000 miles. Thus in a single year, in addition to its housekeeping duties, the individual pectoral sandpiper, a bird weighing less than three ounces, flies the equivalent of seven times east-west across the United States.

In this essay I will describe only some of more common of these shorebirds.

Easily the most familiar of the shorebirds is one of the plovers: the killdeer. It is among the few species that spends the summer in this region. More often heard than seen, its loud *killdee killdee* call speaks most of its name as the bird flies up from an open meadow. Easily identified by the two black bars across its throat, this is a bird you often come across as you walk along a country path. It nests on the open ground and draws you away from its well-camouflaged eggs by walking off drooping a wing as though it is injured.

Once you know how to identify the killdeer, another plover is easy to pick out. It is the semi-palmated plover. It is similar to the killdeer but smaller and has only one of those black neck bars. It doesn't nest here but is rather common here during fall migration.

The other three shorebirds that do nest here are the American woodcock, common snipe and spotted sandpiper. The woodcock and snipe belong to that category of big noses that I wrote about in essay 23. They are retiring woodland birds not easily found, but the spotted sandpiper is a familiar bird most often observed feeding among the rocky shores of local creeks. This species is easily identified not by its plumage — only springtime adults have spotted breasts — or even its distinctive *peet peet peet* call, but by its distinctive nervous teetering motion. It also has a noticeable flight: what my Sibley guide describes accurately as "brief bursts of fluttering wingbeats followed by glide."

Now I turn to those migrants. To do so I will take you on three field trips. The first is to a broad open area at the Iroquois National Wildlife Reserve near the feeder dike. Much of the area is exposed mud, partly covered with a few inches of water and with a background of short grass and cattail fringes. It is a hot morning in mid-August and we'll have vision problems created by moisture drawn up from the water by the bright sun.

This setting is literally filled with shorebirds. It is difficult to announce a count because a dozen will rise and wheel back and forth before settling again in a different spot. Then another group picks up and flies in perfect formation, every wing tipped in synchrony as the birds turn. These maneuvers outdo those airshow fighter pilot displays. In any case there must be at least sixty shorebirds here.

There are a few killdeer and two semi-palmated plovers to give us a start in identifying the species. With them recorded we turn to the others.

Bigger ones first. These are the yellowlegs. And taller would be a better term, because their bodies are only slightly larger than those of the other birds, the appearance of that larger size due mostly to their long yellow legs. There are two yellowleg species: the greater yellowlegs and the lesser yellowlegs. Very similar in appearance they are easiest differentiated by their flight calls. The lesser's calls are paired notes; the greater's in threes.

Now the tiny ones. Really tiny. These birds, called peeps by birders, each weigh less than an ounce. They are like chickadees among robin-sized birds. Here again there are two species to distinguish and this time we do so easiest by the color of their legs: the semi-palmated sandpiper has black legs and the least sandpiper has yellow legs. (The word palmated means webbed. The toes of the semi-palmated plover and the semi-palmated sandpiper are each partially webbed, clearly not an observable field mark.)

We now have picked out six species and we must turn to birds many of which are more difficult to identify. Their size is between that of the yellowlegs and the peeps and I'll help with only a few. The easiest among them are short-billed dowitchers. Two of them are probing deep into the mud with their heads bobbing like sewing machines as they jab for buried insects. Another of these middies is a species I think of as a kind of solid citizen. It is the pectoral sandpiper whose travels I noted. There are several of them. They always appear to me as a bit more plump and slower moving than the sandpipers dashing about them. A slightly smaller bird is the dunlin. Fortunately for today's identification, the one I point out is a juvenile with some black on its belly. At this time of year the adults don't offer this clue.

Our second field trip is to the Bird Island pier that reaches out from the Niagara River toward Lake Erie. There we find on the pier-side rocks two distinctive species, the almost white little sanderling and the harlequin of shorebirds, the ruddy turnstone, whose dark necklaces even after its bright coloration is gone make it an easy identification.

The final visit takes us to an open field between Tillman Park and the New York State Thruway. Here we are very fortunate to find two lovely plovers: the black-bellied plover and the American golden-plover. These birds are twice the size of the killdeer and appear quite similar at this time of year. I know them apart in flight because the black-bellied plover shows a black armpit as its wings rise.

Last but far from least, we see a lone upland sandpiper, standing on one of the white vents that allow gas to escape from the buried garbage here. This bird of open country is now rare here as these extensive grasslands disappear.

59. Colorless

White, black, gray and brown.

White snow and ice, black tree trunks, gray clouds and branches, brown grass and cattails. Not a dab of primary color brightens the dreary landscape. The just rising sun only subdues the deep gray of the cloud cover in the eastern sky.

I think about this as I cross-country ski along the dike that splits the western marshes of the Iroquois National Wildlife Refuge. It is a cold, crisp morning and pinpoints of snow fall like sparks from tree limbs.

Wildlife contributes no additional hues. A lone black starling flies off. A brown deer points its black nose at me, flicks its white tail and bounds away into the dark woods. Fox and turkey tracks are gray against the snow. Little white, gray and black chickadees and gray and white nuthatches search the tree trunks. A cotillion of arguing black crows passes overhead, their raucous caws cutting into the pleasant silence of the morning. A black vole peeks out at the base of a gray-stemmed dogwood, then quickly pulls back into its tunnel.

My approach sends a pair of shy pileated woodpeckers into the air ahead of me, but from beneath and behind them their black and white bodies hide their red crests.

Neutral colors — I don't know who came up with that designation. They really represent absence of color. Except for the hints of brown the morning is like black and white television with its range of what computer manufacturers call gray scales.

As I glide along, I think of anthropologist Oliver Sachs' collection of essays, *The Island of the Colorblind*. In his book Sachs describes a hereditary form of colorblindness called achromatopsia that is disproportionately represented among the people of the tiny Pacific island of Pingelap. The more usual form of colorblindness impairs reception of only a few colors. My friend Roy Callahan, for example, cannot differentiate red and green, creating problems with traffic

signals. But the Pingelap residents lack all color perception.
They live in a world of those gray scales.

A world that is just like this morning as I cross the marsh.
However, even lacking color and with their leaves curled up
or blown away, many wildflowers are still identifiable.
Twisted chicory stems bear little knobs at each joint. Queen
Anne's lace racemes are depleted but still intact. The prickly
pods of wild cucumber swing delicately in the light breeze.

Gray milkweed shells are cracked open and are bare of all
but a few of their feathery seedlets. I stop to send a final one
on its way drifting like another snowflake. Cattail heads are
disintegrating into fluff for their own kind of seed dispersal.

Tall yarrow spikes stand like widely separated sentinels,
one of them overseeing a tangled group of teasels. I see only a
few burdocks, but by the end of the morning my socks will be
covered with them and a few beggars' ticks as well.
Despite the absence of color, I enjoy the quiet morning. To me
this day represents the zero, the starting point of the natural
year. It will be just days before life — and excitement — will
return with a vengeance. Early tree swallows will patrol the
open water. The first robins will appear where snow has
disappeared from lawns, not those drab overwintering birds
but the big Labrador subspecies with its bright orange breast.
Soon spring peepers and chorus frogs will add a sound track
to this still marsh. Great skeins of geese and ducks will span
the blue skies.

And when those days arrive, our lives will be enriched
once again by a full palette of color. For now, however, I am
quite satisfied with this more subdued environment.

60. SPCA

The little merganser dived after a minnow and unfortunately followed its prey into the enclosed water intake at the Huntley Power Plant on the Niagara River. Now it swam desperately to avoid being sucked by the swift current against a screen where it would suffocate. Trapped, its chance of survival was essentially nil.

Ted Janese found it there when he made his last inspection of the area late one afternoon. He and his Niagara-Mohawk co-workers Fran Gunning, Bill Stratman and Mike Galas, stayed on after their shift ended to extricate the valiant bird but, try as they might, they couldn't free it.

End of story?

Not quite. Concerned about the ill-fated merganser, Janese went in early the next morning to check the intake area. To his surprise he found the duck, near exhaustion but still struggling pitifully to stay away from the metal grate. Alerted by phone, Gunning brought in a large minnow net. With it the men were able to rescue the fatigued bird.

A male red-breasted merganser is one of our most attractive ducks. It is the same size and has a green head like a mallard but it would never be mistaken for that species. A slimmer bird, it has a thin, serrated bill, which gives mergansers their alternate name — sawbills. This one gobbled the dozens of minnows the men provided until its crop bulged and a fishtail hung from its mouth.

A call to the S.P.C.A. brought wildlife rehabilitation program administrator Diane Obusek to care for the merganser. She examined it, treated the leg that had abrasions from rubbing against the cement wall of the intake, continued to feed it and finally released the anxious duck back into the Niagara River.

I didn't see the happy conclusion to that story, but I joined Ms. Obusek and Jeff Everett at the foot of Sheridan Drive to watch them release a rehabilitated great blue heron. The disoriented bird had been dug from the snow on a suburban rooftop and cared for until it was now ready to return to the wild. Unceremoniously tossed into the air, the feisty heron quickly recovered its aplomb and flew slowly out over the river. Through binoculars I watched it join companions on Strawberry Island. I wonder if they would believe the newcomer's story.

This was my first interaction with the Erie County Society for the Prevention of Cruelty to Animals and I took the opportunity to rejoin the two rehabilitators at their Ensminger Road headquarters.

Clearly this was homework I should have done long ago. It's difficult to express strongly enough my favorable reaction to this remarkable organization that is entirely supported through public contributions. Like many others, I thought of it simply as a place where you visit to adopt a pet dog or cat. It certainly plays that role, but the building is also a state-of-the-art facility for injured animals including wildlife. In one recent year alone, for example, over 1600 wild animals were treated.

Senior Veterinary Technician John Lattimer, who had started the wildlife section six years ago, showed me the operating room where veterinarians like Dr. Michael Bonda perform surgical procedures. It rivals similar facilities for humans.

But the news was not all good. Ms. Obusek showed me their kestrel, screech-owl, red-tailed hawk and bald eagle, each with injuries from which it will not recover. The eagle is one of three shot in the region this winter. Such birds and animals "repay" the Society for their care by appearing in educational programs.

We should be proud of this excellent facility, its fine staff, its many volunteers and contributors and the services they provide.

61. Williamsville Glen

The call came from Peter Yoerg. He was phoning to pass on a Buffalo Ornithological Society "hotline" bird. "There's a white-eyed vireo in the Glen," he said. "I found it near the south end of the picket fence."

And so another rare bird was recorded in the Williamsville Glen. Peter didn't have to say more about the location. Every serious local birder could find the spot he described without further directions.

Peter's observation was added to the data I accumulated over an eight-year period about spring migrants in the Glen. As I entered it in my computer, I noted that one other white-eyed vireo, a southern species that occasionally overshoots its normal breeding grounds to appear here briefly, had been seen there six years earlier.

Since I couldn't get away to look for the bird, I forgot the call until I received an e-mail message from Dave Suggs. Dave told me that he had also found the vireo but he added that he had read in this newspaper that the Sisters of St. Francis are planning to sell their Glen property. "Surely," he said, "we should be concerned about the possible loss of this wonderful natural area."

That was the first I had heard of this. I had missed the *Buffalo News* article and, when I read Dave's note, my heart sank.

Most people think of the Williamsville Glen as the park located on Glen Avenue that is administered cooperatively by the Village of Williamsville and the Town of Amherst. That park includes lovely trees, graceful walkways, broad open lawns and the Ellicott Creek falls where many wedding parties pose for pictures.

But that park only extends about a hundred yards north of Glen Avenue and it does not include the wooded area at the Glen Avenue bridge. Those woods and all of the property along the creek past the Village Glen Tennis and Fitness

Center on Mill Street and as far north as the Park Country
Club fairways belong to the Sisters of St. Francis. It is that area
that birders refer to when they talk about "the Glen." And
unfortunately it is that area that was threatened by further
Amherst development.

Here are some statistics that would mean little to those
who seek to fill in every square foot of green space with office
parks, condominiums or soccer fields. During those eight
years of my data gathering 138 bird species were recorded
there. On May 12, 1991, 73 species were observed in the Glen
— 22 of them warblers. A year earlier an even more
remarkable 23 warbler species were found there in a single
day and on some spring days 150 individual warblers were
tallied. Over the years the species list included olive-sided and
yellow-bellied flycatchers; gray-cheeked thrush; Swainson's,
worm-eating, Kentucky and Connecticut warblers; and the
hybrid Brewster's warbler. Among nesting birds were sharp-
shinned and Cooper's hawks, screech and great horned owls.

Why this property is such a magnet for birds each spring is
a mystery. My guess is that northward moving migrants
swing northeast when they reach Lake Erie to avoid an
overwater flight. When they get to the east end of the lake
many turn to follow the Niagara River, but others swing off to
the northeast and the Glen plays a role similar to that of
Central Park in New York City. After passing over urban
Buffalo it is one of the first woodlands where they can pause
to rest.

Unfortunately statistics like those I have cited have not
deterred developers' bulldozers in the past, but fortunately
this threatening story has a happy ending. Much of the Sisters'
property was purchased by the state and the area is now
designated Amherst State Park. It remains one of the region's
go-to birding areas.

62. Banding Station

In 1899 Danish schoolteacher Hans Mortensen placed aluminum bands on the legs of a few local starlings and storks to assist him in his study of their life histories. Little could he imagine the world-wide popularity of the activity he initiated.

Just three years later Paul Bartsch began banding night herons in the District of Columbia and what the British call "ringing birds" soon spread across this country as well. By 1919 this new type of bird study was so well established that the United States Bureau of Biological Survey, today redesignated the Fish and Wildlife Service, assumed responsibility for supplying bands and maintaining records.

Bird banding today is an avocation that straddles the boundary between hobby and science. Banders enjoy the thrill of holding delicate birds in their hands — suffering those pesky chickadee pecks as a test of their mettle. They are rewarded by hearing of foreign recaptures of "their" birds and they learn a great deal about the birds they band. But at the same time they contribute important information about bird ecology, distribution, migration, longevity, population changes, diseases and life histories.

Last week I visited Elizabeth Brooks' banding station at the Braddock Bay Bird Observatory outside Rochester, one of the premier sites in North America. Birds are banded there from dawn to dusk — nets checked at half hour intervals — from late April to early June and from mid-September to mid-October.

I accompanied Betsy on a round of the nets. Although I had observed this activity many times and was even a licensed bander myself years ago, I remain fascinated by it and I wondered what interesting birds we would find quietly waiting to be removed from the tangle of their soft hammocks.

And many nets did hold interesting birds. We found in succession a Canada warbler (only the second I had seen that year), a swamp sparrow, a magnolia warbler, a hummingbird whose gorget changed in the bright sunlight from black to bright scarlet, a yellowthroat, a grackle and a catbird. Betsy carefully extracted each bird from its mesh spider web and gently placed all but the hummingbird in carrying bags. She is not licensed to band hummingbirds so she simply released it. The feisty bird — no bigger than her little finger — buzzed up to a nearby shrub from which it peered back as if to say, "And you thought you had me. Ha."

Back at headquarters, Betsy and her assistants recorded for later computer compilation the captured birds' weights — the warblers' less than nine grams, about that of a single pat of butter — and several other body measurements before carefully bending an aluminum identification ring around a leg of each bird.

As he had during most of the thirteen years Betsy had operated this station, Bob McKinney of Rochester banded here as well. Regional Audubon Society members knew Bob from his well-attended banding demonstrations at the annual Allegany Nature Pilgrimages. Three hard-working interns helped that year as well: David Bonter, Karen Koehler and Martha Zettel.

Despite the tens of thousands of birds Betsy had banded — well over 2000 at the Braddock Bay station that year alone — she retained her infectious enthusiasm for her voluntary activity. She proudly told me that she had banded two new species that year: Kentucky warbler and rough-winged swallow.

Federal legislators have recently sought to curtail the "misguided efforts of amateur scientists." Surely those critics are unaware of the scientific contributions of "amateurs" like Elizabeth Brooks.

63. Real Schmoos

The resourceful cartoonist Al Capp, whose *Li'l Abner* comic strip appeared in newspapers for many years before Capp died, created an unusual fictional creature he called a shmoo. Shmoos were perfectly designed to serve humankind: they were extraordinarily tame and prolific, they required nothing to raise, when cooked they tasted like steak and they practically jumped into your frying pan.

Capp was a difficult man. Among other things he was a crudely artful male chauvinist and deeply reactionary in his politics, but he was often able to touch our nerves in instructive ways. His shmoos served as a metaphor for our interface with wildlife.

Over the history of civilization — much of it far from civil — there have been a number of real shmoos. We don't have to go to the Island of Mauritius in the Indian Ocean where the dodo was doomed or the Galapagos Islands where ships' holds were filled with giant turtles to find shmoo-like animals and birds. We had several in North America as well.

The penguin-like and equally flightless great auk, whose bodies served fishermen as food and bait and whose feathers stuffed pillows, was last taken from Iceland in 1844 and Martha, the last passenger pigeon, died in the Cincinnati Zoo in 1914. During the 1870s 25,000 passenger pigeons were netted daily and shipped to posh city restaurants in overstuffed railroad boxcars.

One bird that seemed destined to follow these species from abundance into extinction because of its human-serving qualities was the wild turkey. Ornithologists estimate that there were ten million in North America when Europeans first reached these shores. In 1641 at Fort Orange (now Albany) a minister reported "so many turkeys that they came to the houses and hogpens to feed." Another author designated it "one of the most common birds in New England." This was fortunate as those turkeys served as a diet staple for early settlers who were carving a meager existence out of a hostile wilderness.

Here again uncontrolled harvesting finally took its toll. The last New York State 19th century wild turkey was reported from Allegany County in 1844 and the species was extirpated from all of New England a few years later.

But providentially a few reservoirs of wild turkey populations remained in the extensive forests of the Appalachian Mountains. Nearest to us in New York were a few birds in Clearfield County in central Pennsylvania. Even these were threatened by the loss in the early 20th century of their favorite food crop — the chestnut — and by diseases that were traded back and forth with domesticated turkeys. (The barnyard birds are the same species, now bred into waddling but heavy-bosomed relics of their majestic ancestors.)

The lesson was finally learned, however, and hunting regulations were established. It was not too late and the populations slowly grew. Unlike shmoos that never learned, however, turkeys modified their behavior. They became wary birds better equipped to withstand hunting pressure. They adapted to new areas and spread down out of the deep forests to open country. Thriving, their numbers expanded northward, finally crossing our Pennsylvania border into Allegany State Park around 1950.

Buffalo Ornithological Society regional counts in the late 20th Century reflected the repopulation of this biggest game bird. The first returnee was reported in May 1951. By the 1960s there were an average of 11 each year. That number rose rapidly to 60 for the 70s, 92 for the 80s and 212 for the 90s. In 1995 alone almost 700 were recorded.

Shmoo it may no longer be, but the wild turkey is today not only a symbol of our heritage but also of our willingness to learn from one of our many conservation errors.

64. Ed Kanze

Sooner or later every nature writer has something to say about the demise of the passenger pigeon, a story easily simplified: lots to none. There is even a new book about them by Joel Greenberg, *A Feathered River across the Sky*.

But of all the writing about these doomed birds, I found Edward Kanze's prize-winning essay, "In Search of Something Lost," far and away the most compelling. It appears in his book, *Over the Mountains and Home Again.*

Kanze talks his friend Bill Schoch into climbing a mountain in the Adirondacks to visit a summit where passenger pigeons once roosted by the thousands. And here is how this graceful essay continues: "Right from the start, I'm feeling like a Don Quixote who has pressed Bill into the precarious shoes of Sancho Panza. The idea for the hike borders on crazy. For three years, in all seasons, I gazed out across the wilderness from our house near Bloomingdale. Time and again, my eyes found greatest interest not on Whiteface Mountain, rising like a ziggurat on the eastern horizon, nor on Moose Mountain, nearer and wearing a landslide like a crooked necktie, but on a low, little-known peak, forested all the way to the top, named Pigeon Roost."

From there Kanze balances the story of their difficult bushwhack with the sad record of the birds that we wiped out in the early 20th century.

I have never met Kanze, although we have corresponded; however, local entomologist Dr. Wayne Gall has. In fact, Wayne helped Ed survey the wildlife on his Adirondack property by identifying the various life forms in the section of the Saranac River that passes through it. Wayne speaks highly of his friend.

Just who is Ed Kanze. Publicity blurbs list him as "author, naturalist, photographer and Adirondack guide," but that falls far short of his vita as in each category he excels. His writing has won awards from the John Burroughs Association and the

International Regional Magazine Association and among his six books is one about his travels with his wife Debbie through Australia and another about their travels in New Zealand. And he has written over 1300 newspaper columns.

As a naturalist Kanze served as a ranger and historian for the Gulf Islands National Seashore, for the National Park Service in Maine, Florida, Mississippi and South Dakota, and as a field instructor for the National Audubon Society.

His professional photography has appeared widely and today he continues to lead individuals and groups through the Adirondacks.

I spent a few pleasant hours recently reading Kanze's book, *The World of John Burroughs,* which he also illustrated with his photographs. I am especially glad that I did, because it is not only an outstanding book but it changed my attitude toward Burroughs.

Some years ago I set out to read some of Burroughs' writing. I got halfway though *Wake-Robin,* one of his first and most famous books — and quit. I found his flowery, old style writing too much for me. I was put off by passages like: "The dandelion tells me when to look for the swallow, the dogtooth violet when to expect the wood-thrush...."

But Kanze places Burroughs in a better perspective: as an extremely important contributor to the nascent conservation movement who captured the attention of the public of the early 20th century including seemingly everyone from schoolchildren to leaders like president Theodore Roosevelt, inventor Thomas Edison, financiers Henry Ford and Harvey Firestone and fellow conservationist John Muir.

Of course, Kanze quotes Burroughs in this book, where I find him easier to take in small doses; however, Kanze's own prose I far prefer.

65. A Lake Ontario Winter Census

Dawn was breaking as I walked across the lawn toward Pavilion 4 at Hamlin Beach State Park. The effect was eerie: I could barely make out the building in the half-night on shore, but out over Lake Ontario everything was clear and the day was underway. To beat first light I would have had to come a half hour earlier.

It was a dreary December morning, heavily overcast with a strong wind. Whitecaps marched in rank after rank only to dissolve in spray at the sandy shore. The temperature hovered near freezing, the wind chill still lower. Despite my many layers of clothing, I shuddered as the cold worked its way down my back.

Michael Lanzone was already at work. Only partly sheltered by the building, he turned from his scope to type data into a portable computer. Finishing as I approached, he turned and offered his hand: "Welcome to the Hamlin Lake Watch."

I couldn't help it. My first thought was: So this is the Pied Piper of Hamlin. His association with our regional waterfowl had been as close as the original piper's was with that village's rodents.

Lanzone was hired by Braddock Bay Raptor Research to record the passage of Great Lakes waterfowl at this station located midway between Rochester and Niagara Falls. He spent every day from mid-September until late December counting species as well as the direction in which the birds flew. Although this station had been manned the previous four autumns as well, this 1997 inland count would be more comprehensive and continues to be considered an ornithological first.

Lanzone brought to his task experience counting seabirds along New Jersey shores and his expertise was immediately apparent to me. As a line of heavy sea ducks pumped past he picked out black and surf scoters from the more obvious white-wings. Then he pointed out a lighter-colored but heavier-bodied king eider flying with them. From another skein of ducks he differentiated a few lesser from the many greater scaup, a skill that I have never mastered despite years of trying.

The map of Lake Ontario looks like an oval stretched east to west, but the shoreline is not as even as it appears at first glance. East of Hamlin it turns slightly southeast and the park serves as a corner that waterfowl bend past. Even so most of them fly well out over the lake and it takes good eyes — far better than mine — to identify them even with high powered telescopes. My eyes watering in the wind, I watched several hundred long-tailed ducks Lanzone identified that were so far offshore that they looked like an insect swarm.

Long after my visit the season counts were tabulated and the totals are remarkable. Almost a third of a million birds. Over 35,000 loons about equally divided among common and red-throated; 230,000 ducks, geese and swans; 33,000 gulls, most of them Bonaparte's; 104 jaegers; 57 phalaropes. And, as might be expected from hundreds of hours of observation, several rare species: a gannet, 2 harlequin ducks, a Ross's gull and a marbled murrelet.

Most of the birds, Lanzone tells me, flew east to west — directly into a strong west wind on the day I visited. This is the regular flyway of the delicate Bonaparte's gulls that I was watching as they coasted over the waves. They will turn south along the Niagara River and drift on down Lake Erie as the winter turns harsher. Many scoters now winter near Hamilton in Canada where they feed on the abundant zebra mussels now well established there. The gannet usually migrates along the Atlantic coast but was probably driven down the St. Lawrence flyway by a Nor'easter.

Not only science was well served by this project. Local birdwatchers learned from the data when best to seek out rare species.

66. Wish You Were Here

I call them "Eat Your Heart Out" stories.

With only the faintest signs of spring evident on the Niagara Frontier — a few early red-wings displaying at marsh fringes and a grackle visiting our feeder — a "friend" returns from some exotic place to tell you about the unusual birds he or she has seen.

This is one of those stories and I will try to give non-birders a sense of why such an account tantalizes local bird watchers.

On my recent Florida trip Earl Colborn and I spend most of a day at Merritt Island. To most people, that's Cape Canaveral and indeed we could see the huge rocket gantries off in the distance when we entered the National Wildlife Refuge.

At the entrance a dozen black vultures hopped around at the road edge. Like most of the birds we would see, they were so close that binoculars were not needed. In New York a year earlier Doug Bassett had identified a black vulture that joined the turkey vultures wintering in Letchworth Park. Seeing that single bird a quarter mile off across the gorge was worth a trip through a snowstorm for hundreds of upstate birders. We would see over fifty close up on this single day in Florida.

Birding the refuge is simple. You drive along miles of dike roads, each marsh or backwater exposing more birds and often new species. Most spectacular are the waders: the herons, ibises and storks. They are everywhere: standing in the water, meandering along the road, flying over the reeds. And there are so many.

Compare the numbers we observed at Merritt Island with their status here in Buffalo.

First the white birds. Great egret: I do see increasing numbers of these white herons here each year but Bill Watson found the first nest on Motor Island only a few years ago. On Merritt we found 140 of these larger egrets. Snowy egret: I know of very few recent western New York records; Merritt: 85. Wood stork: these awkward birds are seen occasionally along the Atlantic coast north to Long Island, virtually never here; Merritt; 35. Cattle egret: African expatriate wanderers that occasionally make it to New York. We may see a few each decade; Merritt: 30. White ibis: I know of only one or two Buffalo-area records; Merritt: 50.

Other waders. Tri-colored heron: very rare here; Merritt: 35. Little blue heron: another rare fall visitor to New York, usually as an all-white immature; Merritt: 20, almost all adults in beautiful blue plumage. Reddish egret: never recorded here; Merritt: 5. Glossy ibis: the few seen near Buffalo always draw a crowd of birders; Merritt: 250. The number of these striking black birds with their long decurved bills I found overwhelming.

There are other birds as well, none to my knowledge recorded near Buffalo: 25 anhingas, 10 mottled ducks, a clapper rail, 4 royal terns, 5 scrub jays. There are also dozens of fish crows.

Still not sated with these exotics, we drive down to the Arthur R. Marshall-Loxahatchee National Wildlife Refuge. There we spot two species that Buffalo birders would give eyeteeth to record on their home turf: purple gallinule and limpkin. Walking the dike we had to step carefully around huge alligators whose baleful eyes focused on us from trailside.

Since turn about is fair play, I note the absence from the Merritt Island checklist of rough-legged hawk, snowy and long-eared owls, iceland and glaucous gulls, Northern shrike, even chickadee. Horned lark, purple finch, American crow, brown creeper and junco are rarely recorded there.

Florida birders may want to visit Buffalo next winter.

67. Contrasting Reports

Two recent phone calls led me to a beauty and a beast.

The first call was from Bob Brock. It came in late March.

A little background is in order here. At the time this was written the Buffalo Ornithological Society maintained an informal "hot line" to spread the word rapidly among members about unusual birds that occur on or near the Niagara Frontier. This was before electronic communication made notification much easier. The system worked like an abbreviated chain letter: when you received a message, you are responsible to pass it on to two other birders. I was somewhere down in the middle of the list. Bob Brock called me and I in turn called Tom Harper and Bob Lipp. If I couldn't reach either of them, I had to call the next list members, Don Brasure and Gail Seamans. It was a simple system that worked remarkably well.

For me the problem came next. Bob would report a rarity and give accurate directions to locate it. I would go there as soon as I had an opportunity but I would invariably miss the bird. For example (as I recorded in essay 39) Mike Hamilton and I drove to Rochester to look for an ancient murrelet, a seabird never previously reported anywhere near here. It departed minutes before we got there. Another time a varied thrush was seen on Grand Island a half hour before I arrived. I searched for it for two hours before I had to leave. I learned that it reappeared moments later.

My luck has been so bad that I am regarded by my birding friends as a Jonah.

This time, however, Bob reported a lazuli bunting, a rare western species that had shown up at a feeder south of Batavia. My wife and I drove down the next noon and were invited into the home of Don and Virginia Tiede, where we found a dozen other birders. Remarkably, it turned out that Virginia had been my student years earlier. But now all eyes were focused on the beautiful bunting sitting in a lilac bush

just outside the Tiedes' picture window. The same size as an
indigo bunting, this bird's blue was much softer and it had a
cinnamon streak across the breast. Posing for us in the bright
sunlight, it was spectacular.

I was excited about seeing this lovely lazuli bunting, but I
was equally excited about breaking my terrible hitless streak.

The other call came from Michael Olek, president of the
Messinger Woods Wildlife Care and Education Center in
Holland and, with his wife Noreen, among our finest local
animal rehabilitators. Mike had an interesting story to tell.

Just after our late March snowstorm he learned of several
starving turkey vultures. Indeed, when Mike arrived on the
scene he found five vultures too weak even to fly. All were
sitting too high in trees to reach except one which crouched
forlornly on the ground. After a short chase through
snowdrifts, Mike caught this big bird and carried it home
swaddled in blankets. There he and Noreen fed it a
sumptuous dinner of sweetmeats.

Unfortunately, although they are familiar with the habits
of these raptors, they were not at all prepared for what
happened next. Vultures are notorious for defending
themselves by projectile vomiting and, now well fed and
recovering its strength, this bird was no exception. It suddenly
spewed half-digested food all over Mike and the room in
which it was being kept.

Mike said that the disgusting smell was far worse than that
of a skunk and it took days for him and Noreen to clean and
deodorize himself and their home.

The vulture was returned to the wild as soon as the
weather improved. It sailed happily away, oblivious to the
havoc it had created and its good fortune in being rescued by
these devoted — and this time ill served — rehabilitators.

68. Hunter Bander

Each year on October 14 Jerry Farrell changes roles.

Last Wednesday he once again folded up his bird banding nets and got out his gun to join his comrades for the start of hunting season the next morning.

To me Jerry represents the very best of the hunting community. Deeply committed to conservation and the environment, he spends most of each summer in the prairie provinces banding waterfowl for the Canadian government. This year when he completed his hitch, his flight plans were cancelled by an air strike and he had to make the three day, 2000 mile return trip in Fish and Wildlife Service trucks.

More important to us in the Niagara Frontier birding community is Jerry's spring and fall mist netting of bird migrants in a Lewiston woodlot. His accumulated records over 22 years give us some of the most interesting data available about the movements of birds through this area.

I have known of Jerry's banding for many years but first visited his station only last spring. This fall I spent several days with him.

The spring banding that year was a disappointment. Banders across the northeastern United States agreed that it was the worst season they ever experienced. That does not mean that no birds passed through. Rather, the conditions were wrong for banders to capture them. Most bird migrants fly long distances at night and, barring some weather phenomenon like an early morning rain shower, they spread out widely across the landscape to feed quietly during the day. The ideal time for banders and other birders is when the birds accumulate in an area. On those rare occasions dozens of species may be found in a single tree. That spring provided none of those days and most birds slipped through unrecorded — and unbanded.

On the spring day when I joined Jerry, he banded less than a dozen birds in six hours.

The following fall was different, happily confirming our belief that the previous spring was only an unusual blip in migration history. Each morning found scores of birds in the mist nets.

Bird identification in the fall is more difficult than in the spring. Males that were so strikingly marked in spring have molted and now look more like their less colorful consorts. And first year birds — still not in adult plumage — further complicate identification. Because of those problems, many birders — like me, I admit — simply give up and look for them less often in autumn.

But when you band, you have the bird in your hand. It is not flitting about the treetops obscured by leaves or skittering off through the undergrowth. You have a chance to examine each bird closely, to spread its wing and tail feathers to look for distinguishing marks and to take appropriate measurements for comparison with identification guides.

A case in point. Even in spring the Empidonax flycatchers — least, willow, alder, Acadian and yellow-bellied — are difficult to identify. These small gray birds look so much alike that you usually have to hear them sing in order to differentiate them — and in fall they rarely sing at all. One of the most uncommon of these birds is the yellow-bellied flycatcher. When I was with Jerry, he trapped more of them than I had recorded before in a lifetime of birding. I had almost certainly seen them but I could categorize them only to their Empidonax genus. In the hand, however, the distinguishing characteristics were evident.

I wished Jerry a good outdoor experience this hunting season and I looked forward to visiting his banding station again when he resumes that role next spring.

69. State Bird Book

A significant ornithological event occurred in 1998.

Bull's Birds of New York State, edited by Emanuel Levine of the American Museum of Natural History in New York City and with a Foreword by Governor George Pataki, was published. A copy belongs in the library of every bird watcher in this state, from the beginning feeder-observer to the academic ornithologist. Wives, husbands and friends of birders take note.

This is our fifth state bird book. The first, by J. E. DeKay, *Zoology of New York: Part 2, Birds* was published in 1844. Next came E. H. Eaton's two volume, *Birds of New York State* in 1910 and 1914. John Bull wrote *Birds of New York State* in 1974. Unable to play more than a minor role on the present book due to poor health, Bull is honored in its title. The final predecessor to this book was the more specialized *Atlas of Breeding Birds in New York State*, edited by Robert Andrle and J. R. Carroll and published in 1988.

Unlike all but the *Atlas*, the new book was written by a formidable team of 77 authors. Seven of them prepared introductory essays about this state's environmental and ornithological history and about the Federation of New York State Bird Clubs (today renamed the New York State Ornithological Association) under whose aegis the book was developed. These are followed by accounts detailing range, status, breeding and nonbreeding information and remarks about the 451 bird species recorded through early 1997 in this state. What it doesn't include are identification characteristics; it is not a field guide.

Many Niagara Frontier birders contributed species essays to this book. Among them were: Robert Andrle, Robert Brock, Elizabeth Brooks, Thomas Burke, William D'Anna, Stephen Eaton, Charles Rosenburg and William Watson. I was honored to be a member of that group as well. What I find remarkable is the uniformly high quality of each of these brief accounts.

They constitute not only a compendium of information but also a collection of interesting insights.

How was this possible with so many writers spread across the state? Obviously through the discipline that was provided by Levine and his associates, Berna and Stanley Lincoln, both Lincolns having been past Federation presidents. I know about this discipline as each of my own contributions made several trips to and from New York City in the revision process.

An underlying theme that arises from many of these accounts is the change in bird populations due to clearing of the countryside for farmland during the 18th and 19th centuries followed in this century by the return of much of that land to forest. The recent good news for woodland birds like pileated woodpecker is equally bad news for grassland birds like vesper and Henslow's sparrows.

It is difficult to choose from among these fine essays but my favorites are Don Windsor's pieces about those lowly urban birds: rock dove, starling and house (a.k.a. English) sparrow. My vote for best remark is Steve Eaton's about how our premier game bird got its name. "The Spanish first introduced the turkey from America into Europe in the early 1500s. From Spain it spread rapidly as a domestic fowl throughout Europe, but knowledge of its place of origin did not. In the Middle Ages nearly everything exotic was obtained in or through Turkish, or Arabian, territories. Even our corn is still known in the Near East as Turkey wheat. There is little doubt that our bird derived its name from the country Turkey."

The number of species recorded in New York has increased over the years but new birds continue to appear. Number 452 — the lovely lazuli bunting about which I wrote in essay 67 — is the first of those that must wait to appear in the next volume of the series.

70. Benjamin Franklin and the Turkey

By 1784 Benjamin Franklin was an elderly man. He had served in France as ambassador for the past six years and during part of that time he had participated in the protracted peace negotiations with England. Early that year he wrote a long letter to his daughter, Sarah, the wife of Richard Bache, who had followed Franklin as U. S. Postmaster General.

Like so much of what Franklin wrote, it is a charming letter, full of insights and leavened with humor. Its main context is an argument against hereditary nobility for our new country. Some of the flavor of his argument is contained in his comment on the Chinese, among whom "honor does not descend, but ascends. If a man from his learning, his wisdom, or his valor, is promoted by the Emperor to the rank of Mandarin, his parents are immediately entitled to all the same ceremonies of respect...on the supposition that it must have been owing to the education, instruction, and good example afforded him...."

But the section of the letter of interest to naturalists contains his comments comparing the eagle and the turkey. Some, he says, "object to the bald eagle [as portrayed on a particular medal] as looking too much like a dindon, or turkey. For my own part, I wish the bald eagle had not been chosen as the representative of our country; he is a bird of bad moral character; he does not get his living honestly; you may have seen him perched on some dead tree, where, too lazy to fish for himself, he watches the labor of the fishing-hawk; and, when that diligent bird has at length taken a fish, and is bearing it to his nest for the support of his mate and young ones, the bald eagle pursues him, and takes it from him. With all this injustice he is never in good case; but, like those among men who live by sharping and robbing, he is generally poor, and often very lousy. Besides, he is a rank coward; the little kingbird, not bigger than a sparrow, attacks him boldly and drives him out of the district. He is therefore by no means a proper emblem for the brave and honest Cincinnatus of America, who has driven all the kingbirds from our country....

"I am, on this account, not displeased that the figure is not known as a bald eagle, but looks more like a turkey. For in truth, the turkey is in comparison a much more respectable bird, and withal a true original native of America. Eagles have been found in all countries, but the turkey was peculiar to ours; the first of the species seen in Europe, being brought to France by the Jesuits from Canada, and served up at the wedding table of Charles the Ninth. He is, besides (though a little vain and silly, it is true, but not the worse emblem for that) a bird of courage, and would not hesitate to attack a grenadier of the British guards, who should presume to invade his farmyard with a red coat on."

There is, of course, still more to argue for the wild turkey as a representative of this country. For example, turkey was a staple, together with venison, corn and pumpkin, at those harvest feasts shared by the Massasoits and Wampanoags and Pilgrims in the Massachusetts Bay Colony of the 1620s.

It is interesting that both the bald eagle and the wild turkey were nearly extirpated from this country, the eagle by pesticides and the turkey by market hunting. That both have so successfully repopulated our land should add to our reasons for giving thanks each year on the Thanksgiving holiday marking that early communal celebration.

71. Great Horned Owl

There are many common wildlife species that we seldom see or hear. Among these widely distributed animals are owls, bats and flying squirrels.

The reason we rarely meet these neighbors is simple: we don't go out at night anymore. We sit hypnotized before our television sets or, worse, some of us are even afraid to venture out. When I wrote recently about an evening walk through my residential suburb, I was shocked to receive a note from a woman who urged me to stay inside. "Tree limbs can fall on you and there are too many criminals out there," she wrote. While her message certainly represents rather extreme paranoia, I believe that the general attitude, driven by media reports of atrocities, is far too common.

Even when we do leave our homes, we barricade ourselves inside our automobiles — windows tightly closed, doors securely locked. We are no longer afraid of wild beasts out there but the daily litany of mugging reports mislead us, I believe, to fear our own kind.

I awoke well after midnight recently to think about this. And more important to act upon my thoughts. I rose, dressed and walked out into a lovely clear night, leaving behind my wife once again questioning my sanity.

Margaret Louise Park (later renamed Billy Wilson Park) in Baehre Swamp is near our home so I walked over there. I carried no flashlight: there was a full moon and additional light wasn't needed. Except when the headlights of an occasional car temporarily blinded me, I could see very well.

No sooner had I entered the park when I heard the soft baritone of a great horned owl — *whooo wha-whoo who who*. It came from off to my west, from the woods below the three stars of Orion's belt.

It has always seemed to me that referring to this song as hooting or to its source as a hoot owl is misguided for there is a true musical quality to the notes. I expect that they could be best approximated with a bassoon. Cupping my hands over my mouth, I attempted to imitate them and for about twenty minutes the owl and I conversed back and forth. But she never approached. I say she because the calls of male owls are more drawn out and usually consist of six notes rather than the five I was hearing. So Ms. Owl and I did not meet that night. I would only have seen her anyway as a big shape flying in on powerful but silent wings to perch in a nearby tree. And then, unless the moon had illuminated her big yellow eyes, she would only have merged with the other dark shadows among the branches.

Soon my new acquaintance will find a real partner who will not only join her in duets but will also mate with her. Horned owls aren't much at home construction so she will probably use an old red-tailed hawk's nest. They're such early nesters — eggs are often laid in late January — that she might even be finished with her nest by the time the red-tails are ready to use it again next spring.

If they still want to, that is. Skunks are regular menu items for horned owls and their nests usually retain a hearty measure of their odor. The owls are, in fact, ferocious predators. Bent refers to them as "winged tigers among the most pronounced and savage of the birds of prey." Their main entree is rabbit but they also take squirrels, muskrats, fish, mice, snakes, opossums, and even porcupines. They will be delighted to dine on small dogs or domestic cats, so they represent another reason to keep your pets inside at night. Especially in urban areas they are great ratters, over a hundred recently killed rats found around a single nest.

Delighted by my visit with my unseen friend, I walked back home and returned to bed. Mine had been a pleasant venture into the dark and I thought about it contentedly as I quickly fell back asleep.

71. Bird Artist

Fred Szatkowski's Portrait of an Eurasian Vulture

Some years ago four year old Marcella Szatkowski sat on the living room floor of her Depew home intently watching a television nature program. "Look," she suddenly called out, "that's daddy's bird."

When Marcella's younger sister Grace and her parents joined her, they saw on the screen a big Andean condor sailing in the stiff Pacific winds rising over Peruvian mountains. And indeed, an Andean condor was the subject of one of her father Frederick Szatkowski's paintings, "Portrait of a King," that were on display in the Buffalo Museum of Science that week.

This fine artist's work has continued to gain wide recognition. His painting of goldeneyes courting among ice floes in the Niagara River was honored as 1995 state migratory bird stamp, following by just two years Royalton artist Ron Kleiber's similar award. Szatkowski's paintings were also the subject of an essay in *The Conservationist* in February 1996. Even more important, his delicate pencil sketch of cinerous vultures, a remarkable depiction that makes two ugly birds strangely attractive, is now on international tour with the prestigeous Leigh Yawkey Woodson Art Museum's *Birds in Art: 1995*. That achievement alone places him firmly in the company of the finest nature artists in the world.

No one could have stronger local antecedents than Fred Szatkowski. Born in Cheektowaga, a John F. Kennedy High School graduate who studied graphic design at Bryant and Stratton, a former Trico design artist, he served for a number of years as a staff artist at the Buffalo Museum of Science. There he and his colleague Wayne Robbins were responsible for five new or updated dioramas in the "Hall of the Niagara Frontier."

In 1996 Fred walked me through that museum wing. In the lifelike exhibits every detail is carefully presented. Each time I visit I never fail to find another feature that I have missed in the past: a bird foraging in the grass or a caterpillar crawling along a tree limb. But this tour gave me a different insight: how the designer sees his own exhibit. I learned how difficult it is to fit the portrayal into a fixed and unforgiving space: how, for example, curved corners force compromises in what must appear as straight lines and how the diorama designers have to take into account all viewing angles. From the edges of the windows I could see how even the most remote corners of the exhibits were carefully prepared.

Fred's career led him from commercial designer to nature designer and now he continues to add further credentials as a nature artist. The exhibit of his paintings in the museum showed his progress in this direction. There were fourteen paintings on display. Only three are subjects foreign to the Niagara Frontier: the condor, an African crowned crane and a sleeping warthog with an attendant starling that he titled "Hakuna matata." Its meaning, "No worries," is familiar to children from the recent film, *The Lion King*. These last two paintings derive from Fred's African trip taken, he pointed out, "before I was married, of course."

His other museum paintings capture and bring new insights to local scenes. A heron rises awkwardly through early morning mist, a downy woodpecker speculatively eyes a red admiral butterfly, an angry great horned owl seems to hiss at us, three wigeon rest in light snow, a chipmunk pauses over the mushroom he has been eating, two spring peepers contemplate each other across beech leaves, a mourning cloak butterfly poses on nightshade and a goose family swims in evening light.

Today Fred is no longer associated with the Buffalo Museum, which gives him greater freedom to pick and choose his own subjects. An indication of the high quality of his work is his membership in the prestigious Society of Animal Artists. The vulture painting Fred kindly provided to accompany this essay clearly indicates this quality. I usually think of vultures as birds that are handsome at a distance, ugly close up. Fred's portrait is instead majestic.

The Niagara Frontier is well represented by this fine artist.

73. Winter Robins

One of the pleasures of spring is being taken away.

Many of us won't enjoy that special moment in March when we see our first robin of the oncoming season. We will no longer be so rewarded because we will have been seeing robins all winter.

A few robins stay with us every winter but the number has been increasing each year. Christmas Bird Counts reflect this trend. The average New York statewide count of robins in the 1960s was about 1000, in the 1970s almost 3000, in the 1980s just under 5000, all of it in the face of a 15 percent decline in the population of breeding robins across the state.

The winter population has indeed increased but this year's numbers are still extraordinary. I have received more calls about flocks of robins this winter than about any other recent topic. I have seen several thousand myself, mostly along the shores of Lakes Erie and Ontario.

In fact, the phenomenon is not just local. Internet messages from across the state and in particular from Rochester and Oswego cite similar experiences. And a Minnesota teacher is collecting national data about these numbers.

The common refrain is, "Why is this happening?"

It is interesting to speculate and I will do so, but with a major reservation. Like most explanations for natural events, mine will be guesses — guesses based on data and experience, but still guesses.

After the record-breaking cold and snow of January it is difficult for us to recall the protracted fall that preceded it. We had a long, warm and especially dry autumn. In fact, those generally higher temperatures contributed to our lake effect snow in January by keeping Lake Erie relatively warm and entirely ice-free until mid-month.

That mild fall may well have proved too much of a temptation for the robins, delaying their response to the inbred urges that normally pull birds to the south.

Like blackbirds and crows, robins retreat to roosts at night, the size of those roosts increasing through the summer until some wooded areas are filled with thousands of these birds. One a few miles south of Albany contained over 50,000 robins in the late fall and early winter of 1984 and Alan Klonick tells me of a similar roost, not quite as large, south of Rochester.

Perhaps in those flocks, just as there are instinct-driven bird conversations — "Well, fellow Red-breast, it seems like time to head south" — there are also weather-driven responses — "Hey mate, why hurry? There's still plenty of food around and can you beat this warmth?"

Why hurry indeed? Because January was lurking around the corner. Whatever the cause of their delay, it caught impressive numbers of these birds far north of their normal wintering grounds.

I think that we are seeing so many robins near the large lakes because they are retreating along their established spring migration routes. In spring their northward movements are blocked by Lakes Erie and Ontario and most follow the lakeshores east until they turn north again the other side of Oswego.

Whatever the reason for their stay, they are now subsisting mostly on tree fruits. Some of you may have observed a flock in just a few hours stripping an ornamental fruit tree of its berries. Leftover apples in lakeside orchards are also helping.

But an ice storm will threaten them severely. If that occurs, you might put out on the ground bunches of grapes or apple halves. A day or two of that sort of assistance could save some robin lives.

And if you look closely, you can still enjoy your early March pleasure. The first returning robins are the larger, brighter-orange-breasted Labrador subspecies.

It is important to note that this essay was written in the early 1990s. I have retained its original form because it gives you the opportunity to observe that there was then no reference in it to global warming. The data about the number of robins in New York by decades I gathered through use of a program developed for me by University at Buffalo staff. We organized that data for all New York species for use by individual writers in the preparation of *Bull's Birds of New York*. Unfortunately, unlike the June Breeding Bird data compiled by the U. S. Geological Survey Patuxent Research Center, the Audubon data is only available for individual counts and I know of no similar activity since ours. My own observations suggest, however, that the upward trend of overwintering robins has continued apace.

74. Halcyon Days

The Latin name for our belted kingfisher is *Ceryle alcyon*. That essay start surely rivals Bulwer Lytton's (and Snoopy's) infamous "It was a dark and stormy night" as an opener that doesn't encourage you to read on. But at least my reference now in late December is timely.

Timely? Our kingfisher is a rather common summer resident of this region. If you spend a day then alongside any local creek, sooner or later one will come rattling along to give you a quick look at a handsome blue and white pigeon-sized bird with a big bill and a rather ratty hair-do. If you're lucky you'll also see the kingfisher suddenly pause in mid-air, then drop head-first into the water. If successful, it will reappear with a minnow in its beak and fly up to a nearby snag where it will devour its meal.

Midwinter, however, is not when you should wait at streamside. A few kingfishers do stay around the region all year. We usually find one along the Canadian side of the Niagara River during our January first birding tour. But 99 of 100 head south along with many of our neighbors. Why then is this the time to write about the kingfisher?

The reason comes from that Latin species name: *alcyon*. We have an English word that derives from it: halcyon. It is one of those words so favored by college entrance examiners. It pops up often enough in literature to make it a kind of stylish "in" word to appear on tests. For those unfamiliar with the word, halcyon means calm, peaceful, tranquil or, by extension, prosperous.

And I learned some time ago from one of those delightful two-minute *Weather Notebook* segments on NPR that halcyon days have a technical meaning as well: they are the two weeks around the Winter solstice. That means that they occur in the last half of December. Surely someone is joking here: calm? peaceful? tranquil? Not at least here in Buffalo. Snowy and windy, more likely. Indeed, the name was not coined here but in ancient Greece where Mediterranean breezes don't quite match ours coming off Lakes Erie and Ontario.

The association of the kingfisher with halcyon derives from a Greek myth about Alcyone, the god Aeolus' daughter.

Here is how *Weather Notebook*'s Bryan Yeaton tells the story: "She married Ceyx, King of Thessaly, and they were extremely happy. Unfortunately, Ceyx died in stormy seas, and, grief-stricken, Alcyone threw herself into the ocean. But before hitting the water, she transformed into a bird and enfolded Ceyx's lifeless body with her wings. Feeling her deep grief, the gods changed the couple into kingfishers.

"Ever since, the legend goes, Alcyone carries her dead mate to his burial, then builds a nest and launches it out to sea. There, she lays her eggs and hatches her chicks, brooding over her sea-borne nest for seven placid days before the Winter Solstice and seven calm days after. While she broods, Aeolus himself reins in the wind and sea, protecting his daughter and his grandchildren."

Mariners in particular have been taken with that lovely story and continue to predict that those weeks will represent a period of calm weather.

There are, of course, some difficulties associated with the myth. Even in Europe mid-winter is not a time for kingfishers to nest. And, like ours, their kingfishers do not build floating nests but rather dig holes in embankments in which they raise their young. More important, the days that are halcyon among the Dodecanese Islands are not necessarily the same as ours along the Unity Island Pier.

It makes a pleasant story though.

75. Weather and Bird Migration

I give up.

For years I have been trying to interpret weather patterns in an attempt to associate them with the timing of bird migration. I am not alone in this. Every dedicated birdwatcher across North America tries to predict the day when the spring migration will peak so that he or she can take the field early that morning.

It is clear that birds do not return on the same date every year. Close observers report that, despite claims to the contrary, even the famous swallows of San Juan Capistrano in California are irregular in their arrival. Early swallows are disregarded or considered "just scouts." And when the weather is bad in Los Angeles on the arrival date, the missionaries wait until after the storm to look for returning swallows. Here on the Niagara Frontier bird records vary even more widely with arrival dates for individual species differing by as much as a week from one year to the next. Several years ago I wrote an essay about what I perceived to be the perfect weather scenario for a truly big birding day. It went something like this:

Early May weather across the eastern United States is cold and rainy with front after front moving through from the north and west. The jet stream bellies south along the Mason-Dixon Line holding the flood of spring bird migrants at that latitude.

Now suddenly in mid-May, the weather breaks. The jet stream shifts north above the Canadian border, the weather warms and a high-pressure system moves through, closely followed by a low. The air movement between the two cyclonic systems — the high flowing clockwise, the low counterclockwise — produces south winds that release the migrants allowing them to rush north that night in response to their pent-up instinctual drives.

Now one more factor intervenes. After midnight the low pressure moves in bringing rain showers. Migrants, that might have simply flown through, drop into our woodlands to seek shelter and sustenance. And because of that earlier poor weather, foliage is only beginning to emerge. The birds are forced to search for insects among the low shrubs, thus offering good opportunities for observation when dawn arrives to bring out the birders.

Had the year I wrote that been like that? All would agree that it certainly had not. We had week after week of pleasant weather and were way ahead in local degree days, the measure gardeners use to indicate how advanced the growing season is. Not only that but leaves were out in force by mid-month, not at all conducive to birding.

Despite all those empediments to good birding on May 15 that year a team of four local birders, Willy D'Anna, Mike Morgante, Steve Taylor and Mike Turisk, set a new record for bird species seen here in a single day — 170.

Let me place that number in perspective. Even though I have done more birding this year than in many recent years, I had recorded only 143 species by May 15. And that includes some seldom seen here that I picked up in Virginia and Alabama — chuck-will's widow, fish crow, dickcissel and blue grosbeak. My list may not compare with some of our finest observers but it still gives an idea of how remarkable is that single day 170 total.

And as if that were not extraordinary enough, a Cornell Laboratory of Ornithology team — John Fitzpatrick, Steve Kelling, Kevin McGowan, Ken Rosenberg and Jeff Wells — listed 220 species on the New Jersey state-wide World Series of Birding one day count that year, enough to earn them the out-of-state team trophy but only second place overall. An in-state team found 223 species.

So much for my weather scenario.

76. Canada Geese

Since the remarkable crash landing of US Airways Flight 1549 in the Hudson River after striking a flock of Canada geese on January 15, 2009, we've been hearing a great deal about birds causing airplane accidents. The same concern was raised in 1960 when an accident with a less fortunate outcome took place in Boston. How many recall today that episode when a jet hit a bird flock first reported as rare pine grosbeaks but later identified as starlings? That plane crashed wing-first into Boston Harbor and 62 people were killed.

And we're learning now about the preventive measures taken at airports: local bird colonies dispersed, guns and cannons fired to scare them, trained dogs and peregrine falcons employed as chasers. But, as usual, our interest will soon wane, just as it did shortly after that 1960 crash. That is just as well as thankfully such episodes are rare and our aircraft industry doesn't need additional problems at this time.

Instead of reviewing the difficulties with birds that add to the worries of airplane pilots and passengers, in this essay I write about the villain of the recent near-disaster, those Canada geese.

It is hard to realize today that Canada geese were rare birds seventy years ago. Evidence of this is provided by the Buffalo Ornithological Society's May censuses of the Niagara Frontier. In the 1930s no Canada geese at all were found in May and in the 1940s the counts averaged only six. Compare that with the 2000 count when 4271 were recorded. (More geese were reported on the corresponding April counts, but those were migrants, not the resident birds that constitute our major problem.)

As a young birder in the 1940s and 1950s, I joined groups that traveled from Rochester to visit the Oak Orchard Swamps on our annual Easter goose trip. There we were thrilled to see increasing numbers of those Canada geese stopping over on their migration to the far north. Those numbers of migrants peaked in the 1960s and have declined ever since.

In the early 1940s Jack Miner was one of my personal ornithological heroes along with the Craighead brothers and Roger Tory Peterson. Miner was a Canadian birder who had founded in 1904 what came to be known as the Jack Miner Bird Sanctuary in Kingsville, Ontario near Windsor. There he raised and released those rare Canada geese and banded them as well. Miner's bands included, together with the usual instructions to report where the bird was found, Bible verses like: "*Have faith in God.*" *Mark 11:22*; and "*Let us consider one another.*" *Hebrews 10:24.* I suspect that some of those Bible verses provided the grace before the dinners of successful goose hunters.

This unlettered man caught the good will of a continent and books were written about him. To many and especially to waterfowl hunters, he was saving a species. As an indication of his popularity: shortly before Miner died in 1944, several United States newspapers rated him the fifth best known man on the continent after Ford, Edison, Lindbergh and Rickenbacker. He had been presented with the Order of the British Empire by King George VI in 1943 "for the greatest achievement in conservation in the British Empire."

With our current situation, it is no wonder that Miner's popularity waned. How did this rare bird become the too common resident not only of our marshes but of our corporate lawns and golf courses, forcing us to tiptoe across those lawns to avoid their slimy guano and to drive golf balls into herds of them? More important, how did it become the scourge of those marshes that it is today, causing declines in the populations not only of birds like moorhens and rails but of muskrats as well.

Many observers believe that it was a change in diet that not only supported their population increase but also led to their ability to overwinter in the north. They switched from slimy eelgrass to corn, from a low energy value diet to one of the highest available.

There were other factors as well. Poor management has certainly been one of them. Game managers identified at least eight Canada goose subspecies and sought to protect each one. This meant hunting season restrictions to guard their smaller migrating populations. And, of course, with ever fewer hunters even that population control has been reduced still further.

So we are left with another seemingly unsolvable problem. Wouldn't it be great if we could collect, prepare and serve those resident geese in our food kitchens?

77. Gifted Birds

You were brought up more respectably than I was if you have not heard anyone referred to as a "birdbrain." That slang word has even made it into our recorded language. My *American Heritage Dictionary*, for example, defines birdbrain as "a person regarded as silly or stupid." Through my life, I have been too often the referent to forget that word.

In her 2016 book, *The Genius of Birds*, Jennifer Ackerman reminds us of how that attitude relates to the birds from which it is derived. "Our language reflects our disrespect," she tells us. "The expression 'bird brain' entered the English language in the 1920s because people thought of birds as mere flying, pecking automatons, with brains so small they had no capacity for thought at all." But then she adds, "That view is a gone goose," and proceeds in 266 pages of delightful prose to tell us why. Bird lineage may indeed identify them as living dinosaurs but you cannot come away from this book without respecting them for their problem-solving ability, their singing repertoires, their tool using, and their geographic sense. And they show human characteristics as well: eavesdropping, gift giving, deception and manipulation. All this with a nut-sized or even smaller brain.

Of course birds are creatures driven by instinct. Scientists refer to this as their being hard-wired. Their stereotyped lives fit into narrowly defined patterns from which they rarely stray. They do sing, but for most species it is the same refrain — often beautiful to be sure — repeated over and over and over, ad nauseam.

Birds do learn, however. Among the famous Darwin's finches of the Galapagos Islands is one species that learned to pry out insects with a stick, a rare example of tool using by non-humans. On a more prosaic level, birds have also learned — adapted at least — to build nests in man-made shelters and to take meals from increasingly complicated feeders.

But my favorite example of bird learning was reported in the early 1950s by the English ornithologists James Fisher and R. A. Hinde in *British Birds*.

In order to tell this story I have to provide some background for younger readers. Until those paper milk cartons that are used today were introduced shortly after World War II, milk was universally sold in glass bottles. And before milk delivery was curtailed and finally almost completely eliminated since then, those bottles of milk were delivered to home doorsteps or milkboxes by milkmen. When I was a youngster, those milkmen traveled in horse-drawn wagons, but by the 1950s (when I was a milkman myself) the horses had all been retired and trucks were used.

Back to the story. Fisher and Hinde tell about British tits, close relatives and look-alikes to our chickadees, learning to open those glass milk bottles in order to drink the milk. They would prize the paper or tinfoil cap from the bottle by piercing it and prying it up. Having gained access to the milk (or more often the rich cream that rose to the top in those times before so much milk was homogenized) they would drink significant amounts. In a few cases they would steal so much milk that they would slip down the narrow neck and drown.

How did these birdbrains learn this technique? Fisher and Hinde are professional ornithologists so they very carefully hedge their conjectures with the usual "need for controlled studies," but the information they report supports a quite reasonable history.

The first record of this form of milk theft was from a Southampton village in 1921 and maps of later records indicate that the activity spread in geographic circles of increasing radii from there and from two other initiation sites near Manchester and Belfast.

This certainly suggests that individual (gifted?) birds found how to remove these caps, almost certainly through a kind of fortuitous trial-and-error. For example, they may have found a cap-less bottle or a bottle with its cap awry and started from there. Other local birds observed the activities of this avian research scientist and copied it, thus spreading the word through their communities.

The technique was even picked up by other species including two that are too well known to American birders — the house sparrow and starling.

Birdbrain indeed.

78. West Nile Virus

I receive many complaints about crows, not a few of them from my wife. Once strictly birds of the open country, these shrewd corvids have within the past thirty years invaded our towns and cities. They now have local garbage routes down pat and those black bags that are so widely used today provide them with readily accessed smorgasbords. Add to that their early morning alarm clock cawing and you have an enemy of my light-sleeping partner.

But now our crows have an important positive role to play. Let's see how they may serve us.

In the fall of 1999 a number of people in the Queens borough of New York City reported similar flu-like symptoms to their doctors, among them high fever, headache, weakness and upset stomach. Unfortunately the conditions did not respond to antibiotics and almost before the disease was identified, seven of the 62 patients died. Although three of the patients were children, almost all of the 62 were elderly and they shared a personal behavior: they spent afternoons and evenings in their backyards.

At the same time dead birds, most of them crows, began to appear in the city and there was a major die-off at the Bronx Zoo. The zoo's veterinary pathologist described the situation as "raining crows" and she noted that the sick birds "couldn't fly, they had trouble balancing." A total of almost 300 were infected and, while 259 were crows, other species included blue jay, eagle, red-tailed, broad-winged and Cooper's hawks as well as kestrel and merlin, mallard, black-crowned night heron, cormorant, kingfisher, robin and rock pigeon. Meanwhile in outlying counties 25 horses were sickened and nine died. Some dogs were found to carry the virus but showed no symptoms and a single kitten that had been saved from a storm sewer became seriously ill.

The disease was finally identified by epidemiologists as a virus never before recorded in the Americas. It is called West

Nile Virus, a form of viral encephalitis carried by mosquitoes. Encephalitis means inflammation of the brain and the name of this particular strain indicated where it was first identified. For most people affected, the symptoms are like a mild case of flu but, as the 1999 experience made clear, for some elderly or very young people the disease can be deadly. Not only that but, although the disease is widespread in Africa, Asia and Europe, there is still no known treatment. As a result a massive (and controversial) malathion spraying campaign was initiated in New York City.

Colder weather suppressed mosquito activity and gave health authorities a few months to prepare for a second-year outbreak. And sure enough, early in 2000 two crows in Rockland County just north of New York City died of the disease.

The number of identified human cases of West Nile virus in New York dropped significantly that year, however. There were only thirteen. Even with the four in New Jersey and one in Connecticut, that represented a 71 percent decrease from 1999.

But there was less positive news as well. The New York State Health Department posted a map showing occurrence of this disease in various animals statewide. As the summer progressed I watched as that map filled in with reporting counties. Finally and remarkably only Chemung County failed to identify any affliction among wildlife species.

We did not escape this spread in Western New York. The number of species — all birds — identified as carrying the disease by county was: Erie 24; Chautauqua 16; Niagara 5; Cattaraugus 4; Allegany, Wyoming and Orleans 3 each; and Genesee 2. (Of course, those numbers reflected not only the presence of the virus but also the level of investigation by individual county health officers.)

The list of species that were found to have West Nile virus statewide was extensive. The bird list included in addition to 811 crows, lesser numbers of jays; gulls and herons; doves, grouse and pheasants; robins and bluebirds; several hawk species; cormorants and kingfishers; waxwings and starlings. Even our smallest species were represented: several warblers and a hummingbird. Among mammals (as well as the 13 men and women) were 13 horses, 14 bats, 3 rabbits, 3 squirrels, 2 cats, 2 raccoons and a chipmunk.

Until that second year it was thought that the virus is communicated only through mosquito bites. Now it has been established that it may also be passed on without that intermediate vector, in the case investigated, from one crow to another.

There was bad news on the mosquito front as well. Originally the disease appeared to be confined to one or two species that occurred only downstate. Now mosquitoes of four different genera carry it, several of the species indigenous to western New York.

Clearly it was necessary to adapt to the West Nile virus. In doing so we had to confront a challenging concern: Would we give up our hard-fought gains in the pesticide wars to address this new enemy? Thankfully, the answer to that question has been that we would retain those gains, but that was in part due to the fact that after 2000 the media lost interest in the disease.

But West Nile Virus continues to be a serious health risk. The decline in numbers in 2000 was not reflected in subsequent years and the disease spread across the country and into Canada. Although the number of United States human cases never again reached the 9868 of 2003, the disease continues to affect over 2000 cases each year and in 2012 a serious uptick to 5674 cases included 286 deaths.

If you look at the maps provided by the Centers for Disease Control (CDC), you will see that the Eastern United States is no longer the center for this disease. Today it is more often a Midwestern and Southwestern disease with a special focus on southern California and Arizona. But cases continue to pop up here as well.

Health departments and the CDC recommend:

* Eliminate insofar as possible stagnant pools that could be mosquito breeding sites, particularly in old tires. Clean gutters, downspouts, and birdbaths and chlorinate or cover swimming pools.

* If you are outside at night, wear appropriate clothing and (except for infants) apply a DEET-containing repellent.

* Make sure that doors and windows have tight-fitting screens.

But there is one more thing that we should all do and that brings us back to those bothersome crows.

Now they can play an early warning role like the canary in the coal mine. If you observe any unusual dead or dying birds and in particular crows, you should not pick them up but instead immediately report them to your state health department.

79. Seeing Your Own Beak

One of the first things I recall from my initial processing when I joined the navy in World War II was our having to put up with a physical examination, one aspect of which was an eye test. It wasn't a difficult test for me but it clearly was for my friend Bob Forester, who stood next in line behind me. "I'm in trouble here because I'm extremely far-sighted," he whispered. "My near vision is lousy and I don't want to flunk out before we even get started." I worried about Bob, but when we met again later in the day, he informed me that he had solved his problem. "Fortunately," he said, "the doctor left the door open to the room where the exam was given. I was able to memorize the small print from that extra distance."

The distant vision of hawks is like Bob's only much more so: they are extremely far-sighted. They are in fact about five times more well-equipped to make out details than we are. As Natalie Wolchover puts it, "If you swapped your eyes for an eagle's, you could see an ant crawling on the ground from the roof of a 10-story building."

That hawk vision is just one of the many ways bird vision differs from ours. A recent article by Luke Tyrrell and Esteban Fernandez-Juricic of Purdue University describes another aspect. Their paper title states their concern: "Avian binocular vision: It's not just about what birds can see, it's also about what they can't."

Before I go further, I want to clarify what is meant by binocular vision. Binocular means simply two eyed. Think about the difference between binoculars (two eyes) and telescopes (one eye); telescopes are monocular. We enjoy binocular vision because our two eyes are in the front of our faces; so too are owl eyes. Our separate eyes absorb two different "pictures" and the two are joined to provide depth perception, aka three-dimensional vision. (The minor differences in what we see are enhanced in 3D movies.)

But many birds are not like us and owls. Because their eyes are on the sides of their heads, they enjoy much less of this binocular vision. We have some of this monocular vision ourselves. All you need to do to see this is compare how far left and right you see with one after the other eye closed. If you experiment carefully, you will find that you still enjoy almost 90° of binocular vision with another 10–20% of monocular vision at each side.

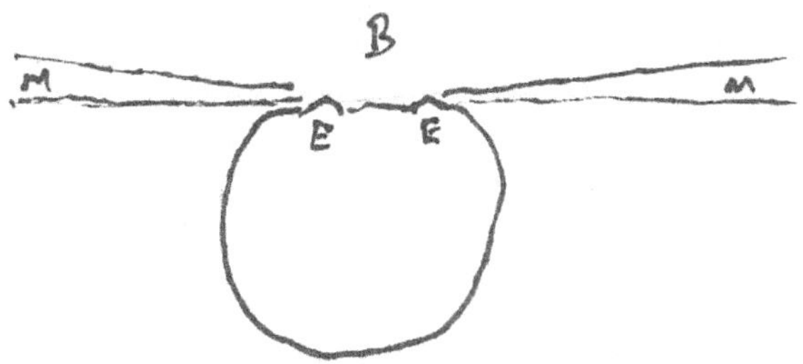

The sketch from above of an owl or human shows this kind of vision when the eyes (E) are in the front of the head with B and M representing binocular and monocular vision. Of course this leads to a large region behind the head that is unseen. But this is reduced simply by turning the head.

On the other hand, because its eyes are on the sides of its head, a pigeon has very little binocular vision, just enough to help it peck at food. It trades this vision for almost 360° of monocular vision — 180° contributed by each eye — which is useful to it for defense: it provides a wider range of vision to detect predators. Unlike them, we — and owls — don't worry about someone sneaking up behind us. The remarkably adapted woodcock actually has full 360° vision and 180° overhead vision as well; it can literally see all around it.

But Tyrrell and Fernandez address still another concern about bird vision: the effect of close-up areas they cannot see. We have a problem related to this: we cannot see our mouths and we have to adapt to this lack. This adaptation provided a laugh on the old burlesque circuit where a clown's attention would be drawn aside just as he prepared to taste an ice cream cone and he would thrust the cone into his ear.

Our noses, like those of owls, don't get in the way, but the noses of many birds do. You can just imagine the problem you would have if you had a heron's beak attached to the front of your face. For many bird species this further complicates the problem of their small amount of binocular vision. They have a blind area not only blocked out by this Jimmy Durante shnozzola but also due to the placement of their eyes on the sides of their heads.

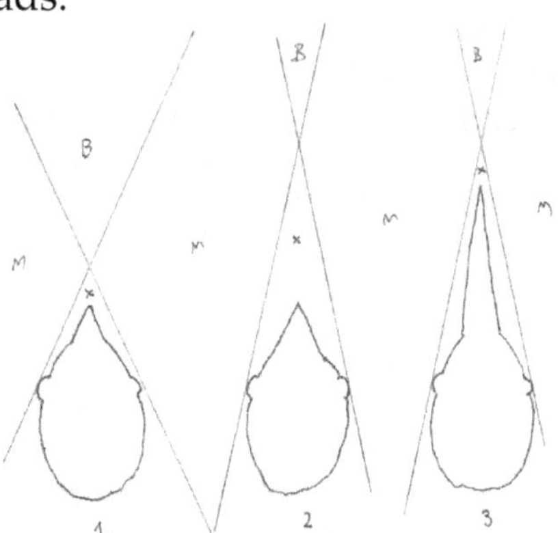

In the second sketch (adapted from one in the Tyrrell-Fernandez paper) are three birds' heads viewed from above with the lines indicating the borders of their vision due to their eye placement. Areas M and B again represent areas of monocular and binocular vision and the area marked with an x represents the area unseen by either eye. (There was essentially no x area on the human-owl sketch.) This is an important region because it can play a role in such activities as locating food or in feeding young birds.

Consider a bird of each type. Bird 1 is well adapted to feeding on fast-moving insects because its blind area is restricted. This is the kind of sight enjoyed by birds like kingbirds and other flycatchers.

Bird 2 would have trouble feeding on such insects because that blind area extends so far forward from its bill. It would feed on slower moving prey or on seeds and berries. An obvious candidate for this pattern is the robin. It is hard to imagine slower-moving prey than the earthworms or underground grubs on which robins feed. And wintering robins feed almost exclusively on berries.

There is something else to notice about robins. If you watch them closely, you will see that they tip their heads to the side. This doesn't improve their binocular vision, of course, but it does give them a better monocular view of the area of ground in which they will soon peck.

Some hawks fit the pattern of Bird 2 as well. Because they attack their prey with their talons, which are much farther from their eyes than are their beaks, they are not punished by this blind area and their binocular vision is important in distant rather than close vision.

The pattern of Bird 3 is obviously fulfilled by a heron, but a woodpecker fits this pattern as well. Notice how the bill fills the blind area represented by Bird 2 leaving only a short distance between the bill tip and binocular vision. Once the bird stabs at its prey, its further actions are determined by tactile rather than visual clues. In woodpeckers, this role is fulfilled by their long tongues.

Many factors add complications to bird vision. For example, species like pigeons use movement of the eyes themselves to gain better perception. For many species, however, the trade-off between binocular vision which aids the search for food and monocular vision that detects predators is complemented by the blind area created by these same trade-offs.

80. Early May: The Silly Season

Each year at this time a few people exhibit strange behavior. Some office workers show up late, slacks oddly creased and stained. They nod through the morning, but then perk up to dash off early at lunchtime.

You could follow one to the gates of Forest Lawn; he returns late again to grumble through the afternoon. Another has a tape recorder in a desk drawer, its wire leading to her ear. Still another whistles oddly foreign-sounding warbles in elevators and hallways.

Out they rush at closing time, their routes directly *away* from their homes.

Meanwhile normally gracious housewives race around markets, push ahead of you into checkout lines and peel out of parking lots to head for local woodlots.

Your first guesses about these people would be wrong. They aren't drug users off to meet contacts, nor are they lovers slipping out to bucolic assignations. And the tape listener isn't a rap fan hooked on atonal iambic couplets.

No, these are bird watchers and they're responding to the spring migration. Long delayed by a tardy winter that has pushed March weather back into May, the waves of migrants are finally passing through and these folks are out to observe again this ephemeral phenomenon.

Those rumpled clothes had been stuffed into boots for an early morning foray into a nearby swamp. The noon cemetery excursion is to look for warblers and a possible orchard oriole in the pink and white blossoms of the pond-lining trees or a red-headed woodpecker along a nearby ridge. The tape recorder is playing bird calls, their nuances being memorized for rapid field identification. And that weird whistling: it is an attempt to improve an imitation screech owl call, used at night to attract this inquisitive owl, in daytime to attract small birds that seek to harry their nocturnal nemesis.

At this season for these folks bird watching turns from a hobby into a sport and it's playoff time for them just as it is for hockey and basketball players.

A local threesome, the Buffalo Zoo team, each year travels to New Jersey to participate in the annual World Series of Birding. Affectionately known as the Bird Nerds, zoo keepers will race around that state for the full 24 hours of an assigned May date to tally as many species as possible. In one recent year the team tallied 114 species, but that only earned them 27th place.

There is a constructive side to their enterprise as well. People participate vicariously in the Bird Nerd adventure by calling the zoo and pledging a penny, nickel, dime or even more for each species that the team tabulates. Those contributions will support that year's designated conservation activity.

Other teams stay to compete within the local region. Each year their total species inch toward 200. In 2002 and 2003 birders in Rochester and then Buffalo surpassed that 200-bird target. To put those numbers into context, recall that boy scouts need only identify thirty species to meet their bird study merit badge requirement.

Also on a designated day in May a more serious count has been mounted annually since 1935 by the Buffalo Ornithological Society. On that day hundreds of birders survey all of western New York and nearby Canada. The accumulated data from those counts provide insights into changes in bird populations.

81. House and Purple Finches

Fred Greanoff of Lancaster, New York wrote to ask a question about feeder birds that had been posed to me several times: "Having had a bird feeder in my yard for many years," he wrote, "I have noticed the decline in the presence of the house finch and purple finch. At one point they were about the only bird present as they liked the black oil seed that I put out. The decline has been over a period of two years to the point now that I never see a one. The sparrows have taken over completely with an occasional blue jay and cardinal. Is this a migration thing, territory take over by the sparrows or just one of those things?"

Before responding to this inquiry, I note that it is easy to confuse house and purple finches for they look much alike. Male purple finches are best described as sparrows dipped head-first in raspberry juice: their heads, breasts and backs are largely rose red. Female purple finches do not show this color and are simply streaked with brown, but the distinctive white streak above their eye separates them from the similarly colored female house finches. The color of male house finches varies from pink to orange and even to yellow but is never truly red and their color does not extend to their backs. (Their color variation is said to be diet related.) The purple finch is by far the less common except in a few Southern Tier locations.

House finches are not native to this region. Their range was originally the western United States but until 1940 they were often illegally captured there and sold in the East as cage birds called Hollywood finches. When this trade was discovered by Fish and Wildlife Service agents, the New York City dealers simply released the birds to avoid prosecution: when the agents came in the front door, the birds went out the back. Remarkably, some of those birds established a Long Island colony and did so well there that they began to extend their new range. I lived in Connecticut in the early 1960s and they appeared at our feeders then. They reached the Niagara Frontier by the mid-1970s and a few years later the eastern and western populations met in the midwest.

These newcomers had a noticeable effect on local populations of house sparrows. Except on farms, the more aggressive house finches displaced the sparrows and the house sparrow population plummeted.

But Mr. Greanoff's observation is on the mark. In the mid-'90s, the house finch population began to decline. The cause: a strain of avian conjunctivitis. First observed in Washington, D.C. in 1994, it spread rapidly among these birds, causing their eyes to become swollen and crusty. This often led to blindness and death from starvation, as the birds could not forage for food. (A more benign form of human conjunctivitis is called pink eye, a disease mostly of children that is often contracted from swimming in polluted water.)

The avian disease is communicated when healthy birds come into contact with an infected bird — as in a crowded roost — or with an object touched by one of them — like those tube feeders on which the bird must stick its bill into a hole in order to extract seeds. When the eyes of an infected bird come in contact with the opening, the next bird to feed at that perch may pick up the disease. For this reason, all feeders should be cleaned with a solution of one part bleach to ten parts water every two weeks or so.

This form of the disease infects poultry and has been detected in a few goldfinches as well. But it is not transferable to humans.

As Mr. Greanoff further observed, the house finch decline was indeed counterbalanced by a corresponding rebound in the house sparrow population.

82. Golf Course Sanctuary

Lawns are wildlife deserts. Suburban yards are bad enough but what are golf courses if not extensive collections of low-cut lawns. Twisting that syllogism to a logical conclusion, environmentalists dislike golf courses.

While they can do little to change their tees, fairways and greens, some country clubs are responding to our — and their — concern for wildlife in other ways. The Tan Tara Golf Club on Tonawanda Creek Road in North Tonawanda is one of them.

In the late 1990s Joe Stein, the Tan Tara superintendent, went through the intensive process of preparing his course for certification as a sanctuary by Audubon International. Audubon International is an organization based in Selkirk, NY not affiliated with the National Audubon Society.

Joe took me on a tour of his course to show me his activities in response to the certification requirements. Many of the fairways were still covered by snow or melt-water so we rode for most of the way in a golf cart along asphalt-paved walkways. Our route took us through deep puddles that I was afraid would short out the cart's motor. It was a sunny afternoon but an icy breeze made me turn up my coat collar. Flying directly into that wind were red-tailed hawks and turkey vultures, early migrants.

The course itself is mostly open with lines of tall ash, maple, oak and even elm trees between fairways. Along its east and west sides are thicker woodlands. A drainage ditch along the east edge is filled with shrubbery; it's a perfect site for songbirds. Joe, whose ornithological credentials were immediately established when he told me that he began his birdwatching with Harold Mitchell, later showed me his species list for the course. His total of 140 was substantially better than the even hundred I had found in Nature View Park directly across Tonawanda Creek.

Next to one of the ponds stood a newly-erected martin house. Purple martins had not yet arrived in this area and we discussed Joe's possible use of taped calls to attract the birds. While we were talking we passed the extensive butterfly garden, now containing only the brown remains of last year's flowers.

Farther out there are many bluebird houses and, sure enough, we found three pairs of these lovely birds already establishing residence. The previous year all of the 14 houses were occupied by ether bluebirds or tree swallows. Nest boxes for bats and at the edge of the woods kestrel, screech-owl and wood duck have also been erected but with less success so far in attracting tenants. A local girl scout troop is monitoring these nest boxes and more are being added each year.

A major change that was surely affecting duffers like me was the grass that constitutes the rough between fairways. Much of it was then being left unmowed. Already, Joe told me, these areas are attracting meadowlarks, bobolinks and savannah sparrows — as well as, I'm sure, complaints from cranky golfers.

Birds were not the only wildlife here. Joe had seen foxes, coyotes, skunks and opossums. Some, like deer, meadow voles and Japanese beetles, represent problems, but strict low toxicity pesticides were being used and those only   when other control methods failed.

Back in his office Joe showed me the six detailed standards he had to meet for certification — environmental planning, wildlife and habitat management, integrated pest management, water conservation, water quality management and outreach and education. He had already filled a full notebook of reports.

This is an excellent program and the Tan Tara Golf Club deserves recognition for meeting these stiff requirements. Other clubs should be encouraged to follow their lead.

83. Dennis Puleston

I had just crossed the Alexandria Bay bridge back into New York from Ontario and was biking southwest along Route 12 in Jefferson County when a large raptor flew a few feet over my head. The big bird sailed up to a messy stick nest perched precariously atop a telephone pole. I rode to where I could observe the adult osprey and its young, scarcely a hundred feet from the highway.

I was struck as always by this majestic fish eagle, but this sighting was no longer an unusual event. Today ospreys are fairly common migrants through western New York and they nest here as well. But forty years ago this would have been a spectacular find.

Through the 1950s the osprey faced extinction. Intensive surveys of the entire Niagara Frontier Region found none at all during half those years and only in the 1990s did a pair return to nest near the Allegany Reservoir.

We can thank one man for the turn-around in the fortunes of this majestic bird. Because of his concern for their declining numbers, Long Island naturalist Dennis Puleston led a coalition of Suffolk County residents, most of them his Brookhaven National Laboratory colleagues, in the initial court battle against the pesticide DDT. Their 1966 suit, supported by watercolors Puleston painted of insects and animals affected by the pesticide, led a local judge to find in their favor.

That landmark decision brought the Brookhaven group national attention. So many calls for assistance were received that they formed the Environmental Defense Fund with Puleston as chairman. Their continuing battle led to a DDT ban in New York and Wisconsin in 1970 and then across the entire nation in 1972. The osprey and the bald eagle were major beneficiaries. Today the Fund has a budget of over $160 million and a membership of 1.5 million.

Much credit for the turn against environmental pollutants is rightly assigned to Rachel Carson, whose *Silent Spring* remains a classic. But it was Puleston and his friends who led the court battles that gave legal status to the movement she started. Their early motto would appeal to lawyers: "Sue the Bastards."

Dennis Puleston died on June 8, 1978 at the age of 95, bringing to an end a truly remarkable life for he was even more than a naturalist and conservationist. He was also a world traveler, an author and painter, and a naval architect. President Truman awarded him the Medal of Freedom for his design of the DUKW, the amphibious landing craft that played an important role in World War II invasions.

Puleston's early life reads like an adventure novel. At 25, he set out on a six-year round-the-world sail in a 30-foot yawl, carrying with him his pet boa constrictor Egbert. In the South Pacific he dined with cannibals, was kidnapped by Espiritu Santa natives, was tattooed with a shark's tooth by Samoans. Captured by the Japanese, he obtained his release by showing his captors a letter of thanks he had received from Emperor Hirohito. He had given the emperor a pair of rare cockatoos.

Wounded by shrapnel in Burma during World War II, he also made it to Normandy where amid the sounds of battle he heard a skylark singing: "I was deeply moved by this one element of sanity in the whole mad business of war," he wrote.

Later he traveled to Antarctica dozens of times. He kept a family pet, a turkey vulture called Alger because it hissed. He wrote and illustrated two books, *Blue Water Vagabond* in 1940 and *A Nature Journal* in 1992, the latter one of my own prized possessions.

Shortly before he died, Puleston told his children: "Please don't grieve for me when I'm gone. It has been a wonderful life and further cause for celebration."

We should indeed celebrate this genuine American hero.

84. Battling Hummingbirds

Hummingbirds are feisty little birds.

That conclusion was underscored for me in Alabama a few years ago when I spent parts of several days watching seven or eight of these combative midgets visiting my brother-in-law's syrup feeders.

I sat on a screened porch looking out over his parched yard into the hundred degree heat, the browns outmatching the greens following almost three years of drought. A half dozen of the trees in the hedgerow that borders his property a hundred yards away had not made it; they stood leafless or with a few remnant brown leaves still clinging to winter-stark branches.

But as far as wildlife was concerned, this could have been a yard in western New York. A cardinal occasionally flew by. Butterflies — cabbage whites, sulphurs, black swallowtails and viceroys — patrolled the lawn. A pair of titmice and a lovely bluebird visited the long-needled pines between this house and the next. A praying mantis sat quietly on a vine that clung to the porch screen. A Carolina wren chortled from the grape arbor. Cone-headed grasshoppers fiddled harshly in the background. And the hummingbirds dashed about with no regard for the heat.

My wife and I have had little luck attracting hummers to our New York State yard. We set out feeders until we decided we were depleting our neighborhood of ants by attracting them to our sugar water. Instead we now put out hanging plants — fuchsias, red as recommended. They are attractive esthetically but they bring us only one or two hummingbird visits a summer. I doubt that we are doing anything wrong; our suburban home simply isn't in hummingbird territory. I see many rural feeders being visited regularly.

In any case, our local failure made me appreciate all the more my brother-in-law's success. Although I site him to make the family connection, it is J.T.'s wife Brenda who cares for the feeders. She has set out three of them, different models of those inverted sugar water-filled glass bowls with their bases circumscribed by fake yellow flowers that advertise drinking tubes.

As nearly as I could determine, there were three male birds, each one having adopted one of the feeders as its personal territory. When not drinking from it, the one "owning" the feeder I watched more often, would sit in a nearby crepe myrtle or high overhead in one of the pines, where it could guard against any interlopers. There it would expose its iridescent red gorget in the bright sunlight. Only adult males sport this brilliant red. The throats of the other birds — females and young — are white.

When one of the other hummers tried to visit the feeder, the owner zoomed in at terrific speed and a dogfight would ensue. How those tiny brains can drive them through such intricate maneuvers is beyond me. Barely inches apart they would race around the corner of the house, swoop back through several Immelmann turns, zoom up fifty or sixty feet into the sky, only finally after perhaps ten seconds of these intricate acrobatics to separate, the male returning to its guard post, the other bird retreating into the distance.

When they passed close by, I could hear the hum of their wings, but this was nothing to the sound of the broad-tailed hummingbirds I have observed in the West. And the ruby-throated hummingbirds make mouse-like squeaking noises. The only other sound I heard from them was a thrum that resulted when one flew into the screen apparently seeking to get through to investigate my red shirt.

I did discover how the excluded birds got to the feeders by getting up at dawn one morning. There in the near dark and before the males were active, all four sipped deeply from tubes at the same feeder.

85. Wandering Birds

Like those wealthy European youths of Victorian times, a number of immature birds wander far from home. Their genetic instructions to move south to escape the oncoming cold not yet well in place, in late summer and fall they head off in all directions instead of flying toward warmer climes with their older and wiser parents. And their roaming across the countryside often takes them well outside their normal range, sometimes thousands of miles outside that range.

If we reconsider history, we can speculate that this was the way bird migration itself developed. The glaciers that brought mile-high ice sheets to this region and cold to most of North America periodically for a million or more years drove all life southward. Then when the ice sheets retreated — the most recent episode about 10,000 years ago — wandering birds like these slowly opened new territories to the north but either moved south again during winters or were wiped out. Slowly and over many generations this accommodation to the changing seasons became imprinted in their genetic memory and migratory behavior was established.

Whether or not that probable scenario represents what happened, we continue to have mostly first year birds wandering far from their normal range in fall and alert bird watchers often record unexpected visitors at this time. From many miles to the west and south have appeared rufous and Anna's hummingbirds, western kingbirds, fork-tailed and ash-throated flycatchers, cave swallows, a rock wren, varied thrushes, Bohemian waxwings, a painted redstart and a black-headed grosbeak.

Occasionally wanderers have even established themselves in our region. When I was a youngster, the cardinal was a very rare bird in western New York. Now it is a common resident and still later arrivals, mockingbirds, already outnumber our native brown thrashers. Birders call species like these half-hardies because severe winters often decimate their populations despite the helpful intervention of bird feeders. Another recent immigrant, the Carolina wren, is one of the birds that has been cyclically beaten back in this way.

The species I have written about so far have all been songbirds but the ones I most often think of as fall wanderers are the herons. The little blue heron is a good example of this. They occur here occasionally in autumn as youngsters in their all white plumage that only later will be replaced by blue and purple of their elders.

The esteemed visitors of 2001 were wood storks. The records of the Buffalo Ornithological Society went back for three-quarters of a century and only twice during those years had wood storks — formerly called wood ibises — been recorded. The first, in 1939, was a single bird seen in a large swamp near Fillmore by two Houghton College professors. The second was in August 1978 when Bob Andrle and others found three near Portville.

Then a report was forwarded that a remarkable 16 of these immature storks suddenly appeared in Wayne County, east of Rochester. It took me two trips but I finally followed directions — a series of lefts and rights on ever-diminishing country lanes — and came upon the birds in a small swamp. They paid little attention to the group of us and we were able to approach within fifty feet.

Despite their featherless, vulture-like heads and their knobby legs, I found these young storks quite attractive. Several were busily seeking fish in the shallow water and they occasionally spread lovely black and white wings, apparently either to frighten their prey into flight or to provide better vision in their shade.

But one thing I missed. None of these storks were carrying babies in diaper slings. That must be their parents' job.

86. Winter Visitors

It is reasonable to believe that unusual birds occasionally occur on the Niagara Frontier during migration seasons, but unexpected species often appear here in winter as well. Here were three rare birds found in this region at the time this essay was written in 2002 — but in each case after a diligent search.

The rarest of the three was the Townsend's solitaire that took up temporary residence in the mixed woodlands of Bond Lake County Park in the Town of Lewiston. The solitaire is an attractive pearl-gray thrush, slightly smaller than a robin. It is easily separated from other gray birds like the catbird and the mockingbird by its readily observed, white eye-ring.

This is a species that summers in the high Rocky Mountain coniferous forests of the western United States, Canada and Mexico. In winter it normally descends to wooded valleys and canyons of the same region. But some individuals wander far and solitaires have appeared along the north shore of Lake Ontario during several recent years. A group of us found one in Canada's Presque Isle Provincial Park several years ago.

This Townsend's solitaire was, however, the first that had ever been recorded on the Niagara Frontier. The bird was most often seen feeding on rose hips and highbush cranberries along the path between East and West Myers Ponds, but its appearance even there was sporadic. It took three visits, each involving long searches of the park, before Mike Galas and I finally found the bird.

Quite unlike the well-named solitaire, a dozen sandhill cranes were being seen regularly feeding in cornfields west of Fredonia. The big cranes were so evident that the only problem locating them was finding the right field.

These too are western birds although a few summer as far east as Manitoulin Island in Lake Huron. Small numbers are seen locally each year during migration periods, but I know of none recorded here in winter before this. Sandhill cranes are often confused with great blue herons. Seen through binoculars, however, the adult birds are easily distinguished by their bright red crown. Also cranes in flight hold their necks extended while herons usually crook their necks into an S-shape to hold their heads just before their wings.

Since the time this essay was written, however, sandhill cranes have been added to the breeding avifauna of western New York. They have chosen the Iroquois National Wildlife Refuge as a nesting area and today it is not uncommon there to hear their familiar bugled call, to see one or more of them fly overhead or to observe several feeding or displaying in one of the refuge marshes.

The last unusual visitor was another western species, a California gull. Its name to the contrary, this is a bird of the interior plains west of the Rockies. It only spends its winters along the Pacific coast.

There is a statue of California gulls erected by the Mormons in Salt Lake City. It honors these birds for coming to the rescue of the early settlers by attacking a crop-destroying plague of locusts.

For several years a single bird of this species has wintered in the Niagara Gorge between the Robert Moses and Sir Adam Beck power projects. It provides still another problem for those who wish to observe it.

The difficulty this time is picking this bird out from hundreds of other gulls in the gorge that differ from it very little. In size this adult California gull is midway between ring-billed and herring gulls. Its mantle (back and wing covers) is darker than those species. It also has yellow legs like the ring-billed gull but red rather than black on the bill like the herring gull.

Our local Chambers of Commerce should be delighted to have birds like these visiting this region for they attract hundreds of birders to the Niagara Frontier from all across the eastern United States and Canada.

87. Two Attractive Sparrows

For birdwatchers sparrows pose identification problems and there are several sources of this difficulty. First, there are many sparrow species. I count ten that are common in one season or another here in western New York and three others that are uncommon or local in occurrence. This listing does not even include the ubiquitous house or English sparrow that is an only distantly-related weaver finch. Second, the plumage of several of these sparrows is quite similar. And third, many sparrows are shy birds that give the observer only fleeting glimpses.

In this essay I do not undertake to distinguish that baker's dozen of species. Rather, I discuss two especially handsome sparrows that pass through this region each spring and fall on their way to and from their breeding grounds in the far north. These attractive birds are easy to identify once you know a few distinguishing features.

In his Bent life history account of the white-crowned sparrow, Roland C. Clement perfectly characterizes this bird: "The white-crown has long had the reputation of being an aristocrat among the [sparrows]. His neat attire, striking crown, and his habit of stretching his head upward to look around have probably combined to earn him this title." Indeed, this species calls to my mind words like neat, elegant, dapper and well groomed.

This species' name provides its best field marks: the bright white stripe over the top of its head and another through its eye are accented by paralleling black stripes. The more common white-throated sparrow has similar markings but has yellow in that second stripe and also, as its name suggests, a bright white throat. The white-crown also has a pink bill. Both species have plain breasts and white wing-bars.

But you don't even need those characters to separate these two birds. The white-throat doesn't enjoy the good posture of the white-crown. It is more mouse-like as it scurries about the undergrowth. You need then only remember the white-crowned sparrow as a sparrow with bright white head markings and excellent upright stature. Even the less elegantly marked females that accompany the males I have described here are easily distinguished from other species by their posture.

The other handsome species is the fox sparrow, a large sparrow strongly marked with stripes that are variously described as rufous, rusty, or reddish-brown. The background for these stripes is gray on its upper parts and white on its breast. Its tail is solid rufous like the hermit thrush. For those who know our common resident song sparrow, the fox sparrow is simply bigger and more brightly colored. Just as you separate the white-crowned sparrow from other sparrows by posture, you distinguish this bird by its brighter color.

Neither of these species breeds anywhere in New York State. Their summer range is in fact almost identical, a band extending across northern Canada whose southern border passes through Moosonee at the south end of James Bay. But whereas the fox sparrow nests in thickets and forests, the white-crown is a bird of more open areas.

Although a few white-crowned sparrows winter here and visit feeders for sustenance, most of them retreat farther to our southwest. Former Niagara Frontier birder Clark Beardslee reported that in spring many white-crowns migrate through this area from west to east, passing north of Lake Erie and then following the south shore of Lake Ontario to Oswego before heading north. Fox sparrows winter south of the Mason-Dixon line and follow a more standard south-to-north migration route.

Look for these attractive sparrows on your lawns or at your feeders this spring. You'll be well rewarded when you see them.

88. Big Year

How many bird species occur here? This is a question I am often asked and I provide some responses in this column. It turns out that there is no single answer and even those answers change.

Until 2013 the total number ever recorded here was 395 species, but that includes three extinct birds: Eskimo curlew, passenger pigeon and Carolina parakeet. In 2013 two species were added to that list, brown booby and elegant tern, so the occurrence list then totaled 397 and the non-extinct list 394. (Note that this essay is about birds in the Buffalo Ornithological Society territory which includes western New York from Batavia west and the Canadan province of Ontario east of Grimsby.)

Can you head out to observe those 394 species? No indeed. Many of those species - like that booby and tern - have occurred here exactly once. In fact only once have 300 species been recorded here in one year: 301 were observed in 2013.

And the most species an individual observer has seen in a year? That record, 283 species, was set in 1962 and held until recently by Richard Rosche. Willie D'Anna set out in 2013 to break that record. He has posted a history of his experience together with photos of many of the unusual species on the web and I draw on that blog to take you through his year highlighting some of the rarer birds. (In parentheses I include his cumulative total through the end of each month.)

January 1: slaty-backed gull, peregrine falcon and Lapland longspur; 2: turkey and black vultures; 3: black-headed gull; 5: red-necked grebe and bohemian waxwing; 6: white-winged crossbill; 12: harlequin duck and red-headed woodpecker; 14: common raven and hoary redpoll; 19: black-legged kittiwake, dunlin, purple sandpiper, little gull and winter wren; 21: Barrow's goldeneye and saw-whet owl; 27: Sabine's gull (103).

February 16 and 17 (after an eleven day holiday trip to New Mexico): greater white-fronted goose and king eider (112).

March 3: evening grosbeak. (D'Anna retired from his role in the state Department of Transportation on March 6); 20: Ross's goose; 31: great egret and tree swallow marking the beginning of spring migration (133).

April 4: Sandhill crane; 6: Eurasian wigeon; 13: American avocet; 14: eared grebe; 15: Forster's tern; 16: pine and black-throated green warblers heralding the beginning of the warbler incursion; 18: Northern goshawk; 23: Western tanager; 24: ruff; 25: trumpeter swan; 29: upland sandpiper and yellow-throated warbler (190).

May 3: golden-winged warbler; 4: willet; 5: summer tanager; 6: glossy ibis; 11: piping plover and American golden-plover; 14: Wilson's phalarope; 16: Eastern whip-poor-will; 19: American white pelican; 21: common nighthawk; 22: whimbrel; 24: snowy egret; 27: clay-colored sparrow (261).

June 2: red crossbill; 4: prothonotary warbler and grasshopper sparrow; 8: yellow-breasted chat; 19: Henslow's sparrow (267).

July 2: sedge wren; 17: stilt sandpiper; 21: sanderling (270).

August 16: Baird's sandpiper; 27: red-necked phalarope (272)

September 2: red knot; 3: olive-sided flycatcher; 9: parasitic jaeger and gray-cheeked thrush; 19: long-billed dowitcher and red phalarope; 23: buff-breasted sandpiper; 28: Nelson's sparrow (282).

October 5: Northern gannet; 7: Brown booby; 8: pomarine jaeger; 18: brant and Pacific loon; 31: Franklin's gull (286).

November 21: elegant tern; 25: lark sparrow (288).

Despite failing to add more species during December, not through lack of effort, Willie D'Anna had set a new record for this region. (His wfe, Betsy Potter, who accompanied Willie on most outings, recorded 283 species herself.) But even so he missed 13 species that were recorded here in 2013. While all are rare birds, several have been seen in the region most years, among them cattle egret, western sandpiper, California gull and dickcissel.

D'Anna's individual accomplishment was, of course, gained with a great deal of technical support, much of it not available to Rosche in 1962. Today all birders have the Dial-a-Bird phone call-in (at 896-1271) managed by Dave Suggs that summarizes the birds seen week by week. BOS members also have a phone Hot Line managed by Mike Galas that reports rarities and provides information about their location and Alec Humann has introduced a resource for smartphones that sends messages to participants, these two resources providing instant communication. Internet mailing lists notify readers of rare birds as well.

89. Suet Feeding

Like Jack Sprat's wife, birds love fat.

And a ready supply of fat can be very useful to them, especially in winter when simply staying alive can prove difficult.

This was brought home to me in striking fashion once when I was banding birds. I weighed a captured song sparrow one afternoon just before the onset of a blizzard. Then 40 hours later I trapped the same sparrow. In that brief period it had lost a quarter of its weight.

Think about that. An equivalent weight loss for a 160-pound human would be 40 pounds. That might seem like an attractive way to diet but it would surely kill you in the process. It's like losing the weight of a leg in a day and a half.

Some studies have also shown that birds have to consume from 50 to 100 percent of their body weight each day. For one carefully observed chickadee this meant capturing and consuming one average-sized insect every 2.5 seconds.

Bird watchers can take advantage of these facts to attract birds by putting out suet for them.

The rewards can be great. Species attracted to suet in this area include downy, hairy, red-bellied and pileated woodpeckers, flickers, chickadees, mourning doves, white-breasted and red-breasted nuthatches, tufted titmice, blue jays, golden-crowned and ruby-crowned kinglets, brown creepers, white-throated, white-crowned and song sparrows, juncos, house and purple finches and of course the omnipresent starlings and house sparrows. Still rarer birds like thrashers, towhees, thrushes, warblers and grosbeaks occasionally visit suet feeders or for tidbits dropped to the ground under them.

Now, while those birds await your catering, let's get down to suet basics.

Suet is animal fat, specifically the fat surrounding the kidneys of cows and sheep. Deer too: hunters take note as birds are especially attracted to deer suet. It is pure and hard and has a waxy appearance. From 15 to 20 pounds can be taken from a single animal.

Years ago butchers were happy to give suet to anyone who asked but today most fat is removed from carcasses at meat packing plants and very little arrives in retail stores. Happily, with birders asking for it, some butchers again provide suet — however, quite reasonably, for a price.

Once you have suet, you can simply hang it out in an onion bag. Most birders prefer, however, to purchase suet feeders. These are hardware-cloth containers with the metal plastic coated so that birds will not injure their bills. I am told that those with roofs seem less attractive to starlings.

My neighbor Ann Fourtner informs me that squirrels are not attracted to pure suet, but that they are to any suet product that has other ingredients added. But I am told that rendered suet still turns away those pesky animals.

To render suet, simply melt it under low heat. To avoid smelling up your house, consider doing this in an electric frying pan in your garage. Once it is melted, you can remove the stringy parts. Then when it is cooled, you can cut it into blocks for feeding. Refrigerate extra blocks in freezer bags. Alternatively, partially cooled suet can be stuffed into crevices in suet logs or pine cones.

Unfortunately, it often takes birds some time to find pure suet. For that reason, many birders stir in other ingredients in various proportions during the rendering process: chunky peanut butter, lard, no-shell birdseed, sugar, cornmeal, flour, raisins or dried cranberries, and even crushed eggshells or sand to help birds digest their food.

Finally, Mike Galas offers a great suggestion: cut a 1.5 inch hole in a coconut, replace the liquid — "drink it, it tastes good" — with a suet mix and hang the coconut out as your feeder.

90. Young Birder

Even after sixty years of birding I occasionally add another species to my life list — a bird, that is, that I have never seen before. Most often those additions occur on trips to other parts of the country: to Michigan for a Kirtland's warbler, to Florida for a scrub jay, to Texas for a curve-billed thrasher, to Alabama for a blue grosbeak, to Colorado for a dipper or to Washington state for a spotted towhee.

Far less often I find a new species on the Niagara Frontier; however, in the fall of 2003, for example, I added a lifer only about a mile from my home in Amherst. There is a story associated with this discovery and I share it with you.

The Nelson's sharp-tailed sparrow (that name now shortened to Nelson's sparrow) is a bird that spends its summers in the prairie provinces of Canada and its winters along our Gulf Coast. As you might expect, the species migrates between those regions along a route far to our west. Occasionally, however, a few of these birds stray east and are recorded in this region.

Two years ago one of these rare sparrows was found by Jack Skalicky in the Iroquois National Wildlife Refuge. I visited the area several times to look for it but without success. This sparrow is very shy and I simply could not find it in the vast cattail marshes of the refuge.

Then early this fall several of our senior local ornithologists suggested that regional birders look for this rare species in small isolated cattail stands.

A neighbor of mine, Jim Pawlicki, took this advice to heart. At that time Jim was a high school student who had been an active birder for only a few years, but he was an alert observer who had learned bird identification remarkably fast.

On a walk along the Amherst bike path between North Forest Road and Millersport Highway Jim noticed just such a small cattail seep a few yards from the trail. He told me later that he thought, "That looks just like what they've been describing as a place for sharp-tailed sparrows." So he investigated and was rewarded. He found one of these rare birds.

When Jim reported his find to the local birding community, my first thought was, "Oh, oh. Here's a youngster who may have, in his eagerness, misidentified a more common bird like a swamp sparrow for this rare visitor. I hope he won't be embarrassed and turned away from this avocation by his experience."

When I arrived at the bike path to check out Jim's find, I met Bill Watson and Bill's news was not good: he hadn't found the bird. However, he added that he might not have looked in the right place.

I asked Bill to return with me and we walked back along the path until we reached the location Jim had described. It was indeed a small cattail patch, a narrow damp slough only about thirty yards long.

When we approached the seep a small sparrow flushed and flew a few yards before it dropped back down in the reeds. Bill got it in his binoculars first and immediately called out, "That's it." I finally picked out the bird where it perched in the reeds and indeed was able to identify the field marks of my first Nelsen's sparrow.

I was, of course, delighted to add this species to my life list. It was number 433, not all that great when you consider my friend Mike Hamilton's list of over 700 species, but still very satisfying.

Even more satisfying was the knowledge that this youngster had outdone all of us old timers.

91. A Border Problem for Birdwatchers

The high security level at the Canadian border initiated after the September 11, 2001 attack that downed two World Trade Center buildings initially created problems for local birders.

On a Sunday morning in January of 2002 Willie D'Anna and Dean DiTommaso walked out along the Bird Island Pier carrying their telescopes. For those not familiar with the Buffalo waterfront, the Bird Island Pier stretches from Unity Island south and parallel to the Niagara River shore. Between the pier and the mainland is the Black Rock Channel, the westernmost stretch of the Erie Canal. Midway along its length the pier passes under the Peace Bridge that connects Buffalo with Fort Erie in Canada. The two bird watchers were looking for a rare species, a shorebird called a willet that had been reported there the previous week.

Near the end of the pier they found the willet and were studying it through their telescopes when they were surprised to hear a shout: "Put your hands in the air and walk slowly toward us." They turned to find three Buffalo police officers, one with a drawn gun pointed at them.

The two birders did as they were told. They produced identification that immediately satisfied the officers, but they were asked to return to the base of the pier to talk with Border Patrol and FBI officials. They were also monitored as they walked back by a Coast Guard boat in the nearby river.

The additional interviews and a search of their car took most of another hour.

A newspaper report of that episode drew reactions that were as mixed as were those on the Internet where Willie described his experience. In fact, the e-mail exchanges became hostile with some responders telling of bad experiences with police (but thankfully not in this area) and others calling the complainers un-American.

My own take on this incident falls between those extremes.

Because Goat Island above Niagara Falls lies within the area that a group of us census several times each year, I have had many opportunities to talk with border guards. I have found them uniformly polite and whenever called upon for information always helpful. When I asked one of them recently, "Have you seen either of the peregrine falcons this morning?" he simply turned and called my attention to the bird I had missed. When he walked on, he left me both thankful and embarrassed.

Although I have fewer contacts with them, I have also been favorably impressed with police officers and customs officials of this area. One Buffalo policeman occasionally calls me to report his unusual natural history observations or to ask questions about local birds.

I invite those who have criticized what they feel was the officers' overreaction in this case to consider how they would have felt walking out onto that pier toward suspected terrorists. They didn't know that the instruments being used were telescopes. In fact, many people I meet believe that a scope I'm carrying is a camera. And if Dean and Willie had been terrorists, they might well have been armed.

So I side with the police on this matter. Perhaps the lengthy wait for the FBI and the car search were unnecessary, but once episodes like this get started, law enforcement officials want to touch all bases.

But now let's consider the future. I hope that birders and our border guards will accommodate each other. One suggestion for birders is to inform the Border Patrol when they will be at the river; another, to seek NEXUS cards to facilitate border crossing and identification.

Today we must recognize that our nation is under threat. This region has even been specifically named because of the power facilities on both sides of the Niagara River. Most border guards and bridge inspectors are already aware of birders but those of us who enjoy this hobby must be prepared occasionally to be inconvenienced.

92. Feeder Survey

In early February 2004 I invited readers who also maintain bird feeders to participate with me in what has come to be called citizen science. I asked them to communicate to me the maximum numbers of each bird species that visited their feeders the week after my *Buffalo News* "Nature Watch" column was published.

Feeder surveys were far from new at that time and mine was based on those carried out by Benjamin Burtt of Syracuse and Allen Benton of Fredonia. I suspect that Burtt's survey was the very first internationally: begun in the winter of 1958-59, it was in 2004 in its 44th year. Later feeder counts were initiated in England in 1970 and at Long Point in Ontario, Canada in 1976. Also, I knew that many readers participate in the Cornell Laboratory of Ornithology national survey that was started in 1987. This local survey was, however, unrelated to the Audubon-Cornell Great Backyard Bird Count of later February.

My invitation continued: "Participants should understand that this is not a contest. Although it will be interesting to receive reports of rare birds, common species like house sparrows and starlings will also provide useful survey information."

Small counts are also important on such surveys. I regularly receive inquiries from readers asking why the numbers of birds visiting their feeders have gone down significantly. The survey would provide more information related to those questions. Did they represent a regional phenomenon or simply local and hopefully temporary aberrations?

Why the timing of the survey? While we were, of course, well past the December 22 Winter Solstice, most birdwatchers would agree that February represents the dead of winter. In only a week or two birds would begin to return, but those smart enough to leave were long gone and those early birds —

the tree swallows and those big, bright-breasted Labrador robins — were not yet here.

Response. Answers to that request for early February feeder counts was both overwhelming and richly rewarding. I received over 270 responses, only a few of which I couldn't use in this summary.

In a follow-up column I thanked everyone for participating. In particular, I noted my special appreciation for the many shut-ins who often shared detailed observations of their feeders. It was humbling to receive their thanks for organizing this task when instead I was in their debt. I wish there was some way of helping these good people to communicate with each other.

What follows is based on 255 reports.

First some general information: A total of 17,628 birds of 58 species were recorded. Only two reports were of no birds at all. Ten were of ten or fewer individual birds and thirty of five or less species. (I suspect that these numbers are not representative as people probably hesitated to report feeders attracting few or no birds.) At the other extreme the maximum number of individual birds reported at one station was 868 and the highest species count was a remarkable 26.

Far and away the most common species reported was the American goldfinch with 2415 observed, 14% of the total. Following it in declining totals were house sparrow, dark-eyed junco, mourning dove, European starling, black-capped chickadee, house finch, Northern cardinal, blue jay and American tree sparrow.

One striking fact about that list stands out: three of the species on it are birds introduced to this area: starling, house sparrow and house finch. Their numbers made up a quarter of the overall total and they visited three-fourths of the feeders.

Although many of the same species occur, the order is quite different for the number of feeding stations at which species occurred. Juncos visited 208 feeders, 82% of them. Others found at over 100 feeders were, again in descending order: chickadee, cardinal, downy woodpecker, mourning dove, blue jay, white-breasted nuthatch, goldfinch, red-bellied woodpecker, starling, house sparrow, house finch and hairy woodpecker.

Those numbers correlate quite closely with the 125 feeder counts in the Dunkirk area recorded by Allen Benton and Dick Miga.

The species that most surprised me was the red-bellied woodpecker. This beautiful woodpecker with its red helmet over white cheeks is a relative newcomer to this area. The numbers of this southern half-hardy were four times as great as its cousin, the formerly far more common flicker.

But the major story of this census relates to hawks. They were reported at 32% of the feeders. This is likely another undercount as many observers only reported birds eating their seeds or suet. Most of the hawks reported were accipiters: Cooper's or sharp-shinned hawks.

Clearly we have created a new niche for predators with our feeding stations. Many reports came in expressing that concern. One was a plaintive, "A Cooper's hawk is taking one or two birds a day from my feeders. What can I do?"

I have no satisfactory answer to that inquiry. Hawks are protected under international treaties and varmint permits are not issued to those who feed birds. One not very satisfactory response is to stop feeding for a period. I promise you that your normal visitors will not starve: there is plenty of food out there. And that temporary break might lead the hawk to seek better territory.

93. Swans

Our three swans are among the most attractive of all waterfowl.

On a recent Palm Sunday over a hundred tundra swans swam about the Cayuga Pool of the Iroquois National Wildlife Refuge. Occasionally a small group beat their wings furiously and paddled rapidly along the water surface until they slowly rose to circle the marshes, maintaining formation as they did so.

In flight their soft *whoo* cries in no way relate to their former name — whistling swans. Nevertheless, seeing these lovely white birds in flight, mournfully crying as they pass overhead, is a moving experience.

For a few weeks each spring and less regularly in fall these lovely birds stop by at Iroquois and attract hundreds of observers to the Cayuga Pool. The pool overlook is on Route 77 between the villages of Alabama and West Alabama.

Tundra swans may also be observed at this time of year along the Canadian side of the Niagara River. Varying numbers stay through the winter in these open waters. In 2004 a record 294 were recorded there on the January waterfowl count of the Buffalo Ornithological Society.

Usually by early April these swans depart for their breeding grounds almost two thousand miles away along the farthest northern shores of the North American continent.

The other two species are more problematic.

The mute swan, a European species, has often been introduced to American parks and private property. As an adult, it is easily identified by its orange bill topped by an overlapping black knob at its base. For several years in the early 1990s one resided at Tifft Nature Preserve until it was killed flying into a power line. More recently an increasing number of pairs have been observed in harbors along Lake Ontario where pairs have also begun to nest.

The mute swan is an aggressive and intolerant species that created serious difficulties around Chesapeake Bay where its population grew from an initial release of five in 1962 to over 3900 in 1999. Human injuries were reported but the swans' disruption of other wildlife is more important to conservationists. They were observed killing many marsh-dwelling birds including ducks and even geese and they also drove away rare nesting terns and skimmers.

Mute swans are also notorious gluttons and at its peak the Maryland population consumed an estimated nine million pounds of aquatic vegetation annually, in the process destroying habitat for crabs and fish as well as birds.

Despite opposition to its program by swan lovers and by the Humane Society of the United States, the Maryland Department of Natural Resources took action to reduce the Chesapeake Bay mute swan population to fewer than one hundred birds. This was accomplished by oiling their eggs and removing (the politically correct term for killing) swans.

A similar program for New York State, where mute swan numbers have increased exponentially was met with such violent resistance that a watered-down version was offered in 2015.

The third swan now beginning to be recorded here is the largest of the three, the trumpeter swan. I consider it the most beautiful bird in North America. Once completely gone from the United States and rare even in Canada, it has now been reintroduced to our northwestern states where it is doing quite well. I was awed a few years ago when I observed three of these swans flying along the Yellowstone River in Montana.

Although most ornithologists agree that this species never bred east of Michigan, a "restoration" program was begun a few years ago in Ontario and another was attempted near the Iroquois refuge. The latter included an attempt to lead the swans to migrate by showing the way with light aircraft. The experiment failed with some birds severely injured in the process and the remaining swans relocated to a Maryland sanctuary.

Although the Ontario birds are non-migratory and, like mute swans, usually respond to hand-outs, they have begun to wander in fall and winter. A few have made it to New York and by the 2000-2005 statewide census six confirmed nests and six other possible nests were recorded.

Many people are glad to see these majestic birds and birders are delighted to add this species to their local lists but, as is the case with the smaller mute swan, these too are voracious eaters and their presence will further endanger our eastern marshlands that are far less extensive than those of the west.

I hope that the future history of mute and trumpeter swans will not replicate that of the Canada goose. Few realize that Canada geese are still uncommon and welcome migrants, but those migrants are now far outnumbered by resident geese that are undesirable pests of golf courses and parklands.

94. Ernst Mayr

Ornithologists around the world celebrated Ernst Mayr's hundredth birthday in 2004. Unfortunately, he would only live for another seven months. He died on February 3, 2005.

This remarkable man — Stephen Jay Gould described him as "the greatest living evolutionary biologist" — began a career in science in 1904 that spanned an entire century. That he lived so long and did so much is amazing, especially considering his early experiences in New Guinea and the Solomon Islands.

Here is how Jared Diamond describes Mayr's early career: "I found it hard to imagine how anyone could have survived the difficulties of the first bird survey of the Cyclops Mountains. That 1928 survey was carried out by the then-23-year-old Ernst Mayr, who had just pulled off the remarkable achievement of completing his Ph.D. thesis in zoology while simultaneously completing his pre-clinical studies at medical school. Like Darwin, Ernst had been passionately devoted to outdoor natural history as a boy, and he had thereby come to the attention of Erwin Stresemann, a famous ornithologist at Berlin's Zoological Museum. In 1928 Stresemann, together with ornithologists at the American Museum of Natural History in New York and at Lord Rothschild's Museum near London, came up with a bold scheme to 'clean up' the outstanding remaining ornithological mysteries of New Guinea, by tracking down all of the perplexing birds of paradise known only from specimens collected by natives and not yet traced to their home grounds by European collectors. Ernst, who had never been outside Europe, was the person selected for this daunting research program.

"Ernst's 'clean-up' consisted of thorough bird surveys of New Guinea's five most important north coastal mountains, a task whose difficulties are impossible to conceive today in these days when bird explorers and their field assistants are at least not at acute risk of being ambushed by the natives. Ernst managed to befriend the local tribes, was officially but incorrectly reported to have been killed by them, survived severe attacks of malaria and dengue and dysentery and other tropical diseases plus a forced descent down a waterfall and a near-drowning in an overturned canoe, succeeded in reaching the summits of all five mountains, and amassed large collections of birds with many new species and subspecies.

"From New Guinea, Ernst went on to the Solomon Islands in the Southwest Pacific, where as a member of the Whitney South Sea Expedition he participated in bird surveys of several islands, including the notorious Malaita (even more dangerous in those days than was New Guinea)."

Mayr described those experiences as fulfilling "the greatest ambition of his youth." He told many stories about his adventures including one of my favorites. He tried to impress some New Guinea natives by using a trick employed by Mark Twain's *Connecticut Yankee in King Arthur's Court*. He learned from his almanac that a lunar eclipse was about to occur and announced to the tribe, through an interpreter, that the moon was about to darken. Unlike the response in Twain's story, however, the natives were not impressed. The elderly chief told Dr. Mayr, "Don't worry, my son, it will soon get light again."

Upon his return from the South Pacific, he spent only one year at the University of Berlin before joining the Department of Ornithology at the American Museum of Natural History in New York City.

While at the American Museum he published his best-known book, *Systematics and the Origin of Species*, which he would later continue to revise and expand. This book created the widely accepted "modern evolutionary synthesis" that combines the theories of Darwin and Mendel and applies evolution not only to animals and plants but to genes at the molecular level. His central concept of species formation was that species populations developed "isolating mechanisms" when they were somehow separated. These mechanisms discouraged interbreeding and allowed the separate groups to become genetically distinct new species.

In 1961 Mayr moved to Harvard where he became Alexander Agassiz Professor of Biology at the university's Museum of Comparative Zoology. Although he continued to contribute to ornithology at Harvard, most of his work there was in more general subjects: evolutionary biology and the history and philosophy of biology.

He won what has been called the triple crown of biological awards: the Balzan Prize in 1983, the International Prize for Biology in 1994 and the Crafoord Prize in 1999. (There is no Nobel Prize for biology.)

Shortly before his death, Mahr was still working. His claim that he would only leave his office "feet first" was nearly fulfilled.

Among the many insights of this outstanding scientist, I offer just one: "Every politician, clergyman, educator, or physician, in short, anyone dealing with human individuals, is bound to make grave mistakes if he ignores these two great truths of population zoology: (1) no two individuals are alike, and (2) both environment and genetic endowment make a contribution to nearly every trait."

95. Short-eared Owls

In 2015 a group of short-eared owls spent the winter in the fields and hedgerows along Posson Road in the township of Shelby, New York.

Shortly after they were first reported, Scott Meier and I drove out to see these birds. We arrived a little after 4:00 p.m. and another birder already there pointed out two of the owls roosting in the hedgerow that ran east from the bend in the road at which we stopped. Among the grass and brush they looked like brown fence posts. When at rest like this they appear about the size of a crow. But owl size is exaggerated by their fluffed-out feathers: a short-eared owl weighs only three-fourths as much as a crow.

Within minutes of our arrival, however, the real show began. The two owls took off and began patrolling the fields looking for voles in the snow. Farther up the road we could see three more in flight. It was hard to believe that these were the same birds we had seen on the ground. Their long broad wings made them appear much larger.

Their flight I find very attractive. Moth-like, they flap, glide and soar only a few feet above the ground, tipping and turning along erratic paths. As I watched these birds I was reminded of shearwaters flying over ocean waves.

When the owls turned away, we could see their nearly white undersides and when they banked toward us their mottled brown backs with light orange patches near their wing ends. Occasionally one would drop to the ground, but while we were there none appeared to find prey.

One owl came to rest in a bush next to the road and we were able to approach in our car to within about twenty feet. We could make out its bright yellow eyes as it alternated peering at us and searching the ground around its perch.

Like most owls (except the hawk owl) short-eared owls are nocturnal or as in this case crepuscular, active at night or in the dim light of evening or early morning. Their eyesight is designed for dimmer light. That is why observers seek them out within an hour or so of dark in evening or morning. The day after our visit I drove down Posson Road in the early afternoon and saw none of these birds.

Other birders had reported harriers in the same area but we saw none. These raptors often feed in the same fields and their appearance is somewhat similar to these owls. The harrier is easily distinguished, however, by a white patch at the base of its tail and its smaller head shape.

On our drive back to Buffalo our conversation turned to the reasons people nowadays rarely see or even hear owls. We came up with many. The owls retreat from our too well-lighted urban and suburban areas. But we provide ourselves few opportunities to interact with them in any case. We seldom venture out at night when we might see them. And we keep our homes sealed in winter to avoid heat loss and in summer to save on air conditioning. Thus we give ourselves no chance to experience the eerie whinnying of screech owls, the shrieks of barn owls, the toots of saw-whet owls or the hooting of barred and great horned owls.

96. Masked Warblers

Who was that masked man?

To those of us of a certain age — very old, that is — that inquiry is a familiar one. It was the penultimate question on the radio show, *The Lone Ranger*. The response was obvious.

I rephrase that inquiry slightly here. My question and the subject of this column is: What is that masked warbler?

Many of my birding friends would respond with a long list of warbler species including golden-winged, chestnut-sided, Cape May, blackburnian, yellow-rumped, cerulean, black-throated blue, magnolia, bay-breasted and black-and-white warblers as well as American redstart and yellow-breasted chat. Among non-warblers, shrikes and waxwings are also masked.

But I think of just two masked warblers: the common yellowthroat and the hooded warbler. The yellowthroat has a black mask that stands out against its largely yellow coloration while the hooded warbler's mask is the reverse: a yellow mask against its black hood. Alternatively you can consider the hooded warbler's yellow "mask" as the eyehole in that black hood.

These two bright little jewels are now among our most common summer resident warblers. Visit any marshy area in western New York and you will hear the cheerful *witchity witchity witchity witch* call of the yellowthroat. Then if you make *shhh* noises, like your school librarians did when you whispered too loud, the little robber will pop up out of the grass or cattails briefly to check on the source of those sounds.

The hooded warbler on the other hand is a bird of the second-growth hardwood forests that have taken over many of our rural areas from what was formerly farmland. As those woodlots have extended, this species has become increasingly common and today I find more of them than I do such woodland warblers as redstart and ovenbird.

This is another species more often heard than seen. Peterson describes its song as *weeta, weeta, weeteo* but I usually hear an additional *ta* at the beginning of that phrase. The similar song of the magnolia warbler rises at the end instead of falling.

Unlike the yellowthroat, however, the hooded warbler is not as easily seen. It doesn't respond as well to those shushing sounds, but a search for the songster is well worth the effort. It is one of our most handsome warblers.

As with so many birds, the females of both species lack the striking coloration of the males. The female yellowthroat has no mask at all but the female hooded warbler has varying amounts of the hood around the yellow mask, so much in a few cases that females have been misidentified as males.

The breeding range of the yellowthroat extends far to our north into Canada but few hooded warblers are found at higher latitudes.

The handsome new edition of Baicich and Harrison's *Nest, Eggs and Nestlings of North American Birds* provides interesting information about these two species. As you might expect their nests conform to their habitats.

The yellowthroat's nest, the book tells us, is "a bulky cup of dead grasses and leaves, ferns, weed stems, bark strips and moss; lined with fine grasses, vine tendrils, bark fibers and often hair" sometimes with a partial covering. It is located "just above the ground or over water, in weeds, reeds or cattails." The three to six eggs are white or creamy white marked with blotches and scrawls that "often form a wreath about the larger end."

The hooded warbler also nests close to the ground, often in a vine tangle. The nest is "a compact cup with a loose outer layer of dead leaves; a main cup of vine-bark strips, plant fibers, weed stems, down and dry catkins lined with plant fibers, fine rootlets and moss fibers." Its three to five eggs are colored similar to those of the yellowthroat.

Both species feed on insects, including such forest enemies as cankerworms and gypsy moths. Yellowthroats usually find their prey on twigs and branches but I often see hooded warblers chasing flying insects.

Like so many of our smaller birds, these warblers are often parasitized by cowbirds. I cringe whenever I see these warbler stepparents feeding young cowbirds that are already more than twice their size.

97. Bird Flu

I have often been asked for information about bird flu, more formally called avian influenza, and I offer this response based largely on an essay prepared for Audubon New York by Richard Haley.

First, some technical information. There are three types of flu virus categorized as A, B and C. Because the B and C types cause relatively mild symptoms in humans, it is only Influenza A that is of serious concern to us. This form is referred to as bird flu because it derives from a natural reservoir almost exclusively in birds. But Influenza A itself comes in 144 sub-types designated by the various forms of two protein molecules, hemagglutinin (H) and neuraminidase (N), located on their surfaces. The type we worry about most often are the various strains of H5N1. One of them killed 60% of those infected.

Those lethal forms enjoy another acronym: HPAI for Highly Pathogenic Avian Influenza. But the terms highly pathogenic and low pathogenic can be misleading. They refer to how lethal the strain is in its normal host: among birds that is. In humans the effect may be very different.

These various virus strains develop as the result of mutations. When a life form replicates, as when we humans have children, the genetic code of the parents is copied and passed on to the offspring. But sometimes the copies are not quite what would be expected. An "error" occurs in the process, like one or more wrong keys being struck on a typewriter. Some mutations are beneficial and in the long-term they may contribute to evolution but others are harmful. Human diseases like Down syndrome, Huntington's disease and cystic fibrosis are the result of such mutations.

Flu viruses multiply much faster than we do and there are many more of them, thus more mutations occur. What we mainly worry about today are: (1) that the bird flu virus H5N1 will mutate into a form that will prove highly lethal to humans, (2) that it will come to where we live, and (3) that it will communicate from birds to humans and then humans to humans.

The first problem is partially addressed by destroying flocks of domestic fowl within which the virus is detected. As to the second, bird flu of any type is rare in the Western Hemisphere and scientists are monitoring wild as well as domestic waterfowl, especially in Alaska where migrating ducks and shorebirds may bring the disease from Asia. We should be thankful that human cases of any form of bird flu have been almost non-existent in North America. The third problem should be addressed by the timely administration of human H5N1 vaccines already being produced but not yet in sufficient volume.

Pandemics are world-wide outbreaks of illness. There were three flu pandemics in the last century: the 1919 H1N1 "Spanish flu" strain: 50 million deaths worldwide; the 1957 H2N2 "Asian flu": 1 million deaths; and the 1968 H3N2 "Hong Kong flu": 700,000 deaths. Although there is no current cure for any flu, many of those deaths were due to complications like pneumonia that improved health care should address. However, even our usual "mild" flu seasons lead to many annual deaths in this country alone. (Because the estimates are difficult to pin down, the reported average annual deaths in the United States from this illness range from less than 500 to 30,000.)

Some important points:

* Thoroughly cooking poultry kills the H5N1 virus.

* There have as yet been no known cases of people contracting the virus from wild birds. The highly pathogenic form of H5N1 among waterfowl has been evident only recently and not here. Still hunters should use increased care in handling any wild animals.

* There is no evidence of danger from feeding birds, but bird feeders should be cleaned regularly to prevent transmission of any diseases.

* Report dead wildlife to the Department of Environmental Conservation only if you find an unusual number. Otherwise their ability to respond to serious problems is reduced.

If the disease does reach North America, domestic flocks in which the disease is identified may be destroyed but culling wild birds has been rejected as creating more problems than it solves.

Bird flu, like West Nile virus (see essay 78), is now a serious but distant threat.

98. What Birds Eat

W. L. McAtee made a significant contribution to ornithology by reporting on the food habits of individual bird species. He did so from before he even graduated from the University of Indiana in 1904, where he spent his entire career working for the United States Division of Biological Survey, today the Biology Resources Division of the U. S. Geological Survey.

McAtee will always be known as the most famous economic ornithologist in the world. No one will ever be able to surpass his accomplishments, because he lived at a time when he could study what birds ate by shooting them and examining their stomach contents. To gain some understanding of the numbers of birds killed for this purpose here are examples of the numbers of a few individual species he and his associates collected and examined: 928 Eastern meadowlarks, 1422 robins and 417 pine grosbeaks.

Many readers today will consider shooting about a half million birds a terrible way to carry out such an investigation, but they should consider three things. First, well into the 20th century the way ornithologists identified birds was "in the hand;" in other words simply shot. McAtee was at least collecting the birds for a purpose. Although bird droppings were also collected and examined, they provided less satisfactory evidence of food habits. Second, there are reasons for the large number of birds studied: he was able to describe food habits at different times of year and in different parts of the country. And finally, do we feel quite as bad about his studies of the diet of mice and rats in this same way?

Whether we like those methods or not, much useful information has been derived from the data. The best source for this information is a book by Martin, Zim and Nelson, *American Wildlife and Plants: A Guide to Wildlife Food Habits*.

Consider for example what we know from the data collected by McAtee and others about the wild turkey. Its most common animal food items are: "beetles, grasshoppers, crickets and walking sticks, ants, wasps and bees, flies (especially Marchflies), crayfish, spiders, snails, millipedes and centipedes, caterpillars and true bugs. There are a few records of salamanders being eaten." And the turkey's plant food: They are "particularly fond of nuts such as acorns and beechnuts (one crop contained 221 large acorns)." but they also consume grape and dogwood fruit in season. Corn and wheat play only a minor role in their diet.

Or consider the great blue heron: 43% of its diet is non-game fish, 25% useful species, 8% insects, 8% crayfish and other crustaceans, 5% mice and shrews and 4% snakes and amphibians. Virtually no plant food is eaten.

Among the interesting conclusions derived from this data, one relates to tree swallows. Birders know this swallow species as the first to arrive in spring. They show up a week or two before barn, rough-winged and other swallows. It is not uncommon to see tree swallows flying over our regional marshes amid late winter snowflakes. Data provided by McAtee and Frank Chapman show that all swallow species except tree swallows feed exclusively on flying insects. But tree swallows eat plant food as well. In fact, in late winter 30% of their diet is botanical. Thus they can get along on plant food before the early hatches of flying insects that are necessary to sustain them and their swallow cousins.

It is especially interesting to examine the information about birds that we now attract to feeders, because McAtee's data were collected before people thought of providing such food. The winter diet of the white-breasted nuthatch, for example, was 68% plant food, largely the fruits of oak, corn and pine. But that percentage dropped off rapidly with no plant food consumed during summer when insects are readily available.

This nuthatch information relates to a question I am often asked: why do birds stop coming to my feeder in spring? McAtee's reports show that many birds turn from plant food, including those seeds you have been feeding them all winter, to insects at nesting time, thus building up their protein resources for breeding.

Shortly before McAtee died in 1961, he contacted me about another of his ornithological contributions. Over his lifetime he had collected bird folk names and I was delighted to publish that information in *The Kingbird*, the state journal I edited at the time.

99. Bird Names

What's in a name? That Shakespearean inquiry applies to birds as well as to the Capulets and Montagues of *Romeo and Juliet*.

There are good reasons for assigning standard names for birds. It can be misleading to have a species referred to by several names. An example of the resulting confusion is the species the Committee on Classification and Nomenculture of the American Ornithologists Union (AOU) and most birdwatchers know as the Northern flicker. My wife and other Southerners call this same bird the golden-winged woodpecker and, as the state bird of Alabama, it is designated the yellowhammer.

We're better off with just one name. However, as the committee itself notes: "Proposals to modify English names are nearly always contentious and involve weighing competing factors to determine whether the changes proposed improve accuracy and clarity sufficiently to outweigh the cost of the instability they would cause."

That AOU committee has responsibility for establishing the currently accepted English names for bird species. The only change one recent report made that affected birds seen locally renamed the rare Nelson's sharp-tailed sparrow simply Nelson's sparrow. That same report added the now accepted French Canadian names for birds: for example, in Quebec the American black duck is canard noir.

Accepting this standardization as a necessary evil as birders and bird book authors follow the current AOU-assigned names. That means changing their check-lists and bird books every few years. It has never been easy for me to make these changes and I often find myself stuttering between old names and new.

There are many reasons for the changes. Sometimes they are made to conform to the names of the same species occurring in Europe. An early example of this was supported by Roger Tory Peterson with his early field guides. He renamed our falcons: duck hawk became peregrine falcon; pigeon hawk, merlin; sparrow hawk, kestrel. The marsh hawk was changed to harrier as well. Those are European bird names, but the changes served another purpose: they each removed the designation hawk at a time when hawks were being hunted nearly to extinction. Of course today they are protected by international law.

Consider a more recent change. The feral pigeons we see regularly were for many years designated rock doves. No longer. Today they are called rock pigeons. This particular change caught Broadway unprepared: the title of a 2007 play was *The Rock Dove*. Perhaps the name change hurt as the play's run was very short.

Sometimes the committee itself cannot make up its mind. It enacts a change and immediately runs into so much flack that it returns the name to the original. Two recent examples come to mind. A common bird of our local marshes was called the green heron for much of my lifetime. The committee changed it to the green-backed heron but the name didn't stick. Thankfully the little bird is again the green heron.

So too the Baltimore oriole was changed to the Northern oriole. Good sense prevailed and it is again the Baltimore oriole, honoring Lord Baltimore's colorful coat of arms. Sometimes tradition wins out.

This same committee also addresses serious issues related to the scientific status of the over 2000 species and subspecies of North American birds. For example, one proposal currently under consideration is to recognize a new crossbill species. That may not mean much to general bird watchers since crossbills are only rare winter visitors to this region from the far north but, if that proposal is accepted, it will add another difficult identification problem for us when they do appear.

Decisions about such matters are increasingly made on the basis of genetic tests. In recent years such studies have resulted in major changes in the assignment of the evolutionary order of birds. For example, until very recently loons and grebes were considered lowest in that order among birds seen in this region. Now they have been moved up past geese, swans and ducks as well as game birds like pheasants, quail and turkeys.

And some name changes reflect politically correct thinking. As I have already noted, the duck formerly called oldsquaw, that name evidently assigned because of the gossiping calls heard from groups of these birds, is now designated long-tailed duck.

Scientists avoid English names in their own formal activities. They use the Latin names that have been assigned to animals and plants since Linnaeus developed the genus species representation in his 1735 *Systema Naturae*. But those change as well. When I was a youngster the robin was Plantesticus migratorius; today it is Turdus migratorius. In that case the bird even migrated to a different genus.

100. Condors

We have a particular affinity for big birds. While small birds like Henslow's sparrows are disappearing from our avifauna, we devote much more of our attention — and corresponding funding — to big birds whose future has been threatened like the whooping crane, the trumpeter swan and the California condor.

There are obvious reasons for this. Little brown birds like those Henslow's sparrows, whose unattractive song is a single *tzelik* and that seldom venture out of their grassland habitat to be seen, don't command our notice. But surely we should not wish to participate in their demise.

Having made the case for the small birds, I admit that I too find myself drawn to those heavyweights. I recall in particular the excitement I felt when I saw my first pair of trumpeter swans flying along the Yellowstone River in Montana, and my similar excitement seeing whooping cranes in the Aransas Refuge in Texas.

But in a lifetime of birding I have never seen a California condor in the wild. There are lots of species I have not seen — my life list doesn't compare with most of my birding friends — but the condor is the one I miss most.

This is indeed a big raptor. Compare its wingspan with our turkey vulture and bald eagle. The span for the vulture and eagle is about six and a half feet; the condor's is nine. Friends who have seen condors tell me that they appear so large in the distance that they are more often misidentified as small airplanes than as eagles or vultures.

That wingspan is the condor's defining characteristic for its 23 pound weight is only about the same as that of trumpeter swans and its 46-inch length is surpassed by whooping cranes and white pelicans.

The 19th century range of the condor extended west of the Rockies from northern sections of Baja California just across the Canadian border into British Columbia, but prehistoric fossils have been found in Texas, Florida and, quite remarkably, at the Hiscock Site in Byron, within 50 miles of Buffalo.

Condors are carrion feeders and their food is almost exclusively the carrion of large mammals: deer, goats, sheep, pigs, cougars, bears, cattle, or even along the coast sea lions and whales.

In the late 19th century there were many reports of dozens of condors and in one case 150 were observed together, but those numbers declined rapidly as the west was settled.

Their association with us has always been a mixed blessing. Condors thrive on the remains of animals shot by hunters, but they in turn were shot and poisoned by ranchers, who thought that they were calf killers. And today their greatest threat is lead poisoning from the bullets they ingest from hunters' prey.

Despite their long lives of up to forty years, condors reproduce slowly and the wild population dropped sharply from about 150 in 1950 to five in 1986. Even including birds kept in zoos there were only 22 living California condors at that time. Any geneticist will tell you that is well below the critical level for survival. At that point despite widespread opposition it was decided that captive breeding was the only route to survival of this species. For their protection the remaining birds were removed from the wild and by 1987 condor survival was entirely dependent on the captive population.

The chance for recovery was extremely slim, especially since until then not a single California condor had yet been raised in captivity. The San Diego Zoo had, however, successfully raised Andean condors and they drew on that experience to work with this northern relative.

Even before the final birds were captured, breeders had found that, if they removed the single egg laid by a female condor, she would breed again. By this means 16 eggs were removed from nests for artificial incubation. Remarkably, 13 hatched successfully. Then in 1988 the first captive pair bred and the program was underway. The hatchlings were raised at various sites including the Buffalo Zoo.

Just ten years later the number of condors had been increased to the 150 birds of 1950 and a release program instituted. As of 2014 there were 421 in the world with 228 of them free-flying in California, Arizona and nearby Mexico. Problems remain but the species appears to be making it. A similar program for the Henslow's sparrow? Not a chance. That species may soon follow its cousin, the Ipswich sparrow, into extinction.

For further information about the condor, see the excellent California Natural History Guide by Noel F. R. Snyder and Helen A. Snyder, *Introduction to the California Condor*.